AF342511

The National Computing Centre develops techniques, provides services, offers aids and supplies information to encourage the more effective use of Information Technology. The Centre co-operates with members and other organisations, including government bodies, to develop the use of computers and communications facilities. It provides advice, training and consultancy; evaluates software methods and tools; promotes standards and codes of practice; and publishes books.

Any interested company, organisation or individual can benefit from the work of the Centre — by exploring its products and services; or in particular by subscribing as a member. Throughout the country, members can participate in working parties, study groups and discussions; and can influence NCC policy.

For more information, contact the Centre at Oxford Road, Manchester M1 7ED (061-228 6333), or at one of the regional offices: London (01-353 4875), Bristol (0272-277077), Birmingham (021-236 6283), Glasgow (041-204 1101) or Belfast (0232-665 997).

Do You Want to Write?

Could you write a book on an aspect of Information Technology? Have you already prepared a typescript? Why not send us your ideas, your 'embryo' text or your completed work? We are a prestigious publishing house with an international reputation. We have the funds and the expertise to support your writing ambitions in the most effective way.

Contact: Geoff Simons, Publications Division, The National Computing Centre Ltd, Oxford Road, Manchester M1 7ED.

Choosing
UNIX
for the Office

An NCC Management Report

R A Barden

PUBLISHED BY NCC PUBLICATIONS

British Library Cataloguing in Publication Data

Barden, R.A.

Choosing UNIX for the office: an NCC management report.
1. Computer systems. Operating systems: UNIX
I. Title
005.4'46

ISBN 0-85012-687-8

First published in 1989 by:

NCC Publications, The National Computing Centre Limited, Oxford Road, Manchester M1 7ED, England.

Typeset in 11pt Century Schoolbook by H&H Graphics, Blackburn; and printed by Hobbs the Printers of Southampton.

ISBN 0-85012-687-8

Contents

Acknowledgements

The author visited many companies and organisations — both user organisations and suppliers of software and hardware — during the preparation of this volume. He wishes to express his thanks to the many people who provided assistance, and in particular to thank the following people for their great help:

Alison Duke of usr/group/UK

Bernard Tissier of Grid Computers

David Saville of Seismograph Services (England) Ltd

Clive Hookins of British Olivetti

Robert Collier of Apricot UK

Robert A Michael of Santa Cruz Operation

Don Folland of CCTA

Tony Renshaw of Wandsworth Borough Council

Brian E Wilson

The Centre acknowledges with thanks the support provided by the Computing Services Committee of the Department of Trade and Industry for the project from which this publication derives.

Introduction

GENERAL

Almost every major hardware manufacturer currently supplies either a version of UNIX, or products based on UNIX. Many other products exploit the UNIX 'look and feel', so that they give a similar outward appearance and similar responses to similar commands. These products are fast becoming the standard non-proprietary multi-user operating systems for mini and mainframe computers. While UNIX has its enthusiasts and its detractors, it is now highly likely that anyone seeking to specify a system for the office environment will consider UNIX as the operating system of choice, or at least as a component of this office system.

This book examines the issues of UNIX which are important to managers and potential purchasers of systems. It sets aside the technical issues, as they are so well covered by a large variety of good-quality publications from several highly competent and distinguished authors. The book considers the achievements of UNIX, and looks at the reasons for and against choosing UNIX, with particular attention to issues that are important to decision makers. Some features of the anatomy of UNIX are described in order to clarify later discussion. Also the standards situation is examined in some detail in order to familiarise the reader with the many different organisations involved with the development and exploitation of UNIX, and also to acquaint the reader with the many versions of UNIX that have emerged.

Market commentators have been claiming since 1980 that UNIX is taking over; in 1988 it seemed that UNIX had finally become acceptable to both buyers and sellers of hardware and software, and that now UNIX machines and software products are being purchased in large quantities. Even with the current confusion of UNIX, Posix and the Open Software Foundation's AIX, the general thrust is towards market acceptance of these products which have been developed from the original UNIX system.

It has often been suggested that UNIX appeals only to academics and hardware enthusiasts who have the time and inclination to tinker with it. However, the substantial sales of UNIX over the past few years indicate that it is attracting buyers from a wide range of disciplines and thus is no longer a graduate's toy. A survey by Yates Ventures in 1983 estimated that, of the 100,000 UNIX sites worldwide, 93% were commercial organisations.

The reasons for the success of UNIX in becoming a major contender for office-systems applications are not necessarily the characteristics of UNIX as an operating system, but are more concerned with the maturity of the user base. Users are now aware that the software for the system is the vital element, and are prepared to search for adequate software rather than simply to buy a hardware package and then look for or write the appropriate software. The huge range of software packages now available under UNIX makes it worthwhile for both user and supplier to pick the operating system that gives access to the appropriate software without the degree of consideration previously given to the make of the hardware.

Success breeds success; so if manufacturers see a positive advantage in selecting one operating system over another they may well fall for its allure. Also, purchasers will try to avoid the pitfalls of pioneering new systems and would rather select the most popular system, where at least some of the worst bugs will have been eliminated.

The success of UNIX mirrors the success of MS-DOS, and for similar reasons. In the early days of the personal computer, manufacturers sought to tie purchasers into proprietary systems by providing unique operating systems. This meant that software purchasers could only select from a range of software which could run under the operating system designed for that single make of machine. Other manufacturers used the readily available, but somewhat quirky, independently developed CP/M, which saved them time and effort by eliminating the need for building their own operating system. Over a period, many hundreds of programs were developed for CP/M machines. Eventually, CP/M was superseded by MS-DOS, which was developed for the emerging 16-bit micros.

The introduction of the IBM-PC was the outward sign of success of MS-DOS, and permitted the development of a huge range of good software. This gave users the choice they needed both of hardware and software, without the usual considerations of long-term support, because both software and hardware were cheap enough to be regarded as short-term expedients. Of course, over the six years since the introduction of the IBM-PC, both hardware and software have been improved; but, if anything, prices have fallen.

It has become increasingly obvious to manufacturers that, by permitting other organisations to design and test software, money can be saved both on development and long-term support for a package. Because it takes so long to develop a new software package this activity is only possible where the software house can foresee the possibility of high unit sales over a period of time. This makes it possible to use the profits from the development of the first package to develop new products or fund extensive improvements to existing products.

The net result of the *de facto* standardisation of an operating system by so many hardware companies is that a large proportion of office functions can be readily implemented using off-the-shelf ('shrink-wrapped') packages. This contrasts with the traditional DP structure of proper, long-term development of in-house systems in that the in-house system is pointed directly at a complete solution of a single company's problems, whereas the off-the-shelf package is intended to tackle some of the problems of a wide range of companies.

The ready availability of the UNIX operating system widens the choice of hardware for the potential buyer, and this allows the buyer to escape from having to select from a single hardware and software portfolio. Instead, the buyer can seek a suitable package among the hundreds available which will cover most of his needs.

Packaged software is relatively cheap and readily obtainable, and the user needs to only spend a relatively small amount of effort in installing and implementing the package. Because the packages are sold to a number of customers there is usually proof that the package functions correctly. The package will be designed to meet a proportion of the user's needs, and the high-quality software available now can often be formatted to approach a more complete solution for the buyer.

UNIX is a multi-user system and thus is acceptable to the manufacturers of minicomputers needing to address the corporate environment and to service complex networks. There can be little doubt that many proprietary operating systems are of equal or better quality than UNIX, but technical merit alone is not sufficient to guarantee success. To quote the classic dictum of Watson-Watt, the developer of radar: 'The best you never get; the second best arrives too late; always go with the third best.' Although this statement disparages the very considerable technical achievement of the developers of UNIX, it expresses the need to set aside the technical merit of a system and to consider only the user's requirements.

UNIX is available over a wide range of hardware sizes, from powerful micros to mainframes, and the portability of the system has often been advanced as a reason for its success. However, few users actually require the same applications programs to run over a range of different types and sizes of machine, and separated by so great a distance that a UNIX-based wide-area network could not cope, or that a conventional large mainframe would not be more suitable. Thus portability in terms of providing software to run on a range of machines may not seem significant to the majority of users. However, development of software on one machine to run on another is commonplace.

The suitability of UNIX for the entire range of office computing is doubtful. At the low cost end of the market, the personal computer is successful, and by its very nature, the PC is not a multi-user device. Also, the PC is becoming a focus for convergence of many office functions, with fax connections, laser printers for desktop publishing, and even telephone answering machines. In this environment, it seems unlikely that UNIX will take over; in fact, the real contest seems to be between MS-DOS and OS/2.

Against this, the development of powerful micros with internal storage of over a megabyte, and with disks holding from 40 Mb upwards, has occurred over the last two years. UNIX, which was intended for mid-range mainframes, and has spread over the minicomputer world, is a powerful contender in the multi-user micro world.

UNIX is unlikely to fit the bill in the giant mainframe arena, where proprietary operating systems, with the accompanying high level of specialist staff, are likely to remain unchallenged because of the huge investment of money and trained staff needed for these systems. But in the departmental office, or the medium-sized company, where computer communications links are needed, or anywhere that package software can be used in an office automation role, UNIX can, and will, find a home. Ultimately, UNIX will also start to take over from the large monolithic corporate systems as existing systems reach the end of their working lives.

UNIX has also the virtue of a good programming language, C, that permits fast construction of software. C is not difficult to use, and provides quick solutions to the traditional problems of acquiring skilled staff and completing a project. A guide to the success of UNIX is the number of job advertisements for C programmers; a year ago there were very few such advertisements in the computer press, whereas now there are many.

This book does not set out to provide a highly technical discussion of UNIX, or details of the compatibility between the many versions and proprietary implementations of UNIX. It still remains uncertain whether a given program could be taken from one machine and run on another make without modification, but that situation is also the same with COBOL; the issue is the use of a common operating system with a range of common facilities. UNIX is succeeding in gaining a substantial market share; it is also succeeding in addressing and solving real business problems.

THE OPEN SOFTWARE FOUNDATION

The launch of the Open Software Foundation (OSF) heralds a new era in the UNIX world. The declared aim of the OSF is to develop a standard operating system which is free from the influence of a hardware manufacturer. To this end a group of manufacturers have put together sufficient funds to establish a body (OSF) to develop and publish this standard. OSF members in June 1988 were IBM, DEC, Hewlett-Packard, Apollo, Siemens, Nixdorf and Bull. AT&T were invited to join, but had not done so at the time of writing (late-1988).

The OSF have an almost unique status in the computing world, with so many large manufacturers contributing funds to products that will hopefully ultimately permit users to select hardware from any supplier that will run a standard operating system. OSF will start from IBM's AIX as a development base, and use X/Open and Posix specifications.

UNIX AND UNIX-LIKE PRODUCTS

UNIX is a trademark of American Telephones and Telegraphs (AT&T), and refers specifically to AT&T's UNIX operating system. There are a very large number of products based on UNIX or with a similar structure; there are many products which present a similar 'look and feel' to UNIX. There are many products with external features such as communications and terminal handling that resemble UNIX. Throughout this book, where a feature is referred to as a UNIX feature it is a part of a version of AT&T's product, and usually later than UNIX System III. However, general comment covers other products than those supplied by AT&T, for example Microsoft's XENIX, so as to provide the widest possible view of the UNIX world; criticisms of particular aspects of this market do not directly describe AT&T's products.

Finally, the author wishes to state that any opinions expressed are his own and are not necessarily those of the National Computing Centre Ltd.

1   Historical Summary

THE BEGINNING

UNIX was created by researchers at Bell Telephone Laboratories. Bell Electric Laboratories is owned jointly by AT&T and Western Electric, and is one of the largest research groups in the world with more than 20,000 employees. UNIX has been evolving over a long period — in fact, since 1965, when Bell Telephone Laboratories were involved in a joint project with GEC and MIT to produce a new operating system. This operating system was titled 'Multics', and intended to be a general-purpose multi-user operating system.

Multics was a multi-user interactive system, giving several users the facilities to independently run programs at the same time on one machine. The interactive aspect gives each user access to the system's facilities virtually immediately, so that each command can be typed and a response obtained. This contrasts with a batch system where all the commands would be blocked together and then executed one after the other with little opportunity for the user to intervene, and then finally all the results will be printed together. Batch systems still reign supreme where continuous running is required to produce the output or for systems where intervention is not required, such as payroll or financial accounts.

The Multics projects started in 1965, but by 1969 there had been little success as far as Bell was concerned in spite of high costs, so the Bell Telephone Laboratories decided to drop out of the project. As Multics had been intended to be the basis for Bell's future products, this left Bell without an operating system, and so the Computing Science Research Centre of Bell Telephone Laboratories were given the task of putting together something to replace Multics.

Multics provided multi-user operation but isolated each user so that groups of programmers working on the same task could not simultaneously use the machine, because each file was linked to a single user as with batch-mode systems. Providing a file structure that separates each user, and yet allows each file to be accessed simultaneously by several users is one of the most important characteristics of UNIX.

Ken Thompson of Bell Labs was working on a project called 'Space Travel', which simulated movement of the planets within the solar system, but the cost of the mainframe time was too great, so a DEC PDP-7 was used for running the program. Unfortunately the PDP-7 lacked sufficient memory to store the source code of the program so the GE-645 running under Multics was used for storage and compilation, then the paper tape holding the new object program was loaded into the PDP-7 for running. The frustration of this process persuaded Thompson to write a new operating system for the PDP-7 that would allow all development work to take place on the PDP.

Thompson, Ritchie and Canaday of the Research Centre developed a file system on paper and a simulator was run on the General Electric GE 645 mainframe that was running under Multics. The system was titled UNIX as a pun on 'single user Multics', and a set of system utilities were cross-assembled from a Honeywell machine to the DEC PDP-7. Thus from the earliest days, UNIX was running across a mix of manufacturers' products. By 1971 UNIX had been installed on a variety of popular DEC minis. In the meantime Ritchie had been developing a new high level computing language, C, and inevitably UNIX was rewritten in C so that it was now possible to port UNIX across to any machine that could run C.

C is relatively simple to use, and system utilities were created for UNIX by many different authors from many organisations, such as universities and libraries.

Early versions of UNIX were used internally by Bell Laboratories, Version 6 becoming generally available in 1976. Version 7 for the DEC PDP-11 was released by Bell Labs in 1978, and licences were cheap enough for many micro manufacturers to port across to personal computers. Many user companies also purchased licences. AT&T sold licences to anyone with £43,000, but provided no support, no maintenance, no warranty and no refunds! In spite of all these disadvantages, a number of companies bought licences for internal use, and it had already become popular with universities in the USA.

Commercial products had been launched by AT&T from 1977, starting with the Programmer's Work Bench (PWB) which was based on Version 6. In 1981 UNIX System III was released, which merged PWB and Version 7 features. In 1983 UNIX System V was released as a fully supported product, with some features derived from a university version, BSD from Berkeley. Later releases (System V.3) included Remote File Sharing (RFS), the streams communications facility and Transport Layer Interface (TLI).

By 1984 there was considerable demand for some kind of regularity of form among proprietary versions, so AT&T developed the System V Interface Definition (SVID) as a method for describing the functional operation of UNIX. This was not intended to provide a strict control over all parts of the system, merely as an easier route to user acceptance by making different versions more familiar.

More and more hardware manufacturers adopted UNIX or UNIX-like products, at least partly because staff from high schools and universities were familiar with the product, and also because there was a growing number of software products from non-hardware organisations. The current release of UNIX from AT&T is UNIX System V release 3.1. Release IV is anticipated for 1989, which is promised to give total conformity with Berkeley and XENIX.

BERKELEY VERSIONS AND OTHERS

AT&T, owners of Bell Telephone Laboratories, were prohibited from selling computer products under a Federal Decree, so they supplied UNIX to universities and similar non-profit making organisations for £200 (or £50 for UK universities). This had the effect of training the next generation of computer specialists in UNIX, as well as providing considerable user feedback at little cost. Many universities and educational establishments became UNIX enthusiasts. The University of California at Berkeley took UNIX Version 7 and adapted it as the BSD (Berkeley Standard Distribution).

This was released as BSD3.2 in 1980. Berkeley also produced the 'vi' text editor, the C Shell and the Ingres relational database system. BSD became very popular with universities, to the detriment of UNIX Version 7, and BSD4.2, which was released in 1984, had even more desirable features, such as Ethernet and TCP/IP (Transmission Control Protocol and Internet Protocol). By 1986 BSD4.3 was available with improved job control facilities and extra communications protocol, and was considered by many universities to be a highly reliable and effective operating system.

By 1984 the BSD products were vying with AT&T's SVID as the latest 'standard', and many user organisations were finding difficulty in deciding which to accept as an internal organisational standard. There are significant differences between SVID and BSD in command names which reflect the different system utilities. The situation has not really been satisfactorily resolved although the recent moves towards international standards have helped to clear up some details. Current release from Berkeley is BSD release 4.3.

It was estimated in 1982 that 90% of US university computer science departments held UNIX licences. The computers used for science and computing also provided administrative and secretarial facilities. UNIX is available in two forms: a source licence from Western Electric which is expensive but can be rewritten and presented as a proprietary product, and as a binary licence which is much cheaper but cannot be readily amended and so is suitable for purchase by a user organisation.

XENIX

XENIX is the result of work by Microsoft on UNIX. The operating system was carefully debugged, then various additional features such as record locking were added in. Finally, a slightly more user-friendly front end was grafted on. Microsoft also carefully re-documented the operating system, an immensely valuable contribution. XENIX has become the most commercially successful implementation of UNIX for micros, used by Altos, Tandy, Plessey and Acorn amongst a host of others.

THE CURRENT SITUATION

At the beginning of 1987 it was estimated by Frost and Sullivan that there were 500,000 UNIX systems worldwide. The author's informal survey suggests that there are about 25,000 UNIX systems installed in the UK, and as each organisation may well have several UNIX systems, there are approximately 15,000 user organisations. About 4500 UNIX systems are in use by central and local government, and by educational institutions.

The Frost and Sullivan report published in 1987 predicted that the UNIX market would grow to 16 times its 1987 size by 1991; with the value of European installations increasing from $1.5 billion at the end of 1986 to $24 million in 1991. The number of European UNIX systems will increase from 40,500 to 677,000. Frost and Sullivan's report emphasised the vital role of standards in making UNIX more attractive to users, and also the feeling in the user community that open systems were becoming more important. The report also mentions the great value of the roles of organisations such as X/Open in resolving standards problems.

As a result of the close collaboration of AT&T and Sun, a major supplier of UNIX hardware, the possibility exists of future versions of UNIX being designed specifically to suit a particular hardware configuration. In this situation, other hardware suppliers would be at a disadvantage compared to Sun, in terms of access to the latest version. A number of manufacturers, including IBM and DEC, have banded together to form the Open Software Foundation in order to produce a 'standard' version of UNIX, probably based on AIX, which will be free of the hardware restrictions potentially to be imposed by AT&T.

AIX is sold by IBM for a range of powerful multi-user micros (IBM 6150) in addition to the 370 series mini/mainframes. UNIX will also be available on the PS/2 series micros. However, AIX was of relatively little importance in the UNIX world until the OSF came along. AIX (Advanced Interactive Executive) definition is a framework for building portable applications for the current ranges of 6150, 370 and PS/2. The Base system is compatible with UNIX V.2 and BSD4.3, and will conform to Posix. Further parts of the system cover ANSI Standard X3J11, graphics based on X-Windows and TCP/IP and Sun's NFS Version 3.2.

2   Why Choose UNIX?

INTRODUCTION

This chapter outlines the reasons why, in the current context, it is worthwhile considering UNIX as a basis for systems for commercial and general use. This chapter tries to avoid technical terminology, and the use of terms which may be unfamiliar to the reader; in any case, such terms are often misused by specialists.

In the main, positive views of UNIX are expressed in this chapter, so as to introduce the reasons why UNIX is becoming successful and point towards why UNIX should be considered for selection. Some contrary viewpoints are also discussed in order to highlight areas where UNIX is unlikely to do well.

Arguments are not presented here in a specific order of priority, as in many cases each point is dependent on, or builds onto, a previous point. For example, UNIX never would have become so popular without being available on a wide range of hardware; nor would so much software have been written for an unpopular operating system. Many points in favour of UNIX are discussed in greater detail throughout the rest of the book, and the interdependence of these points will be clearly seen.

UNIX — LEADING NON-PROPRIETARY OPERATING SYSTEM

Although the heading above sounds like an advertising slogan, it represents the current reality; that UNIX has become the largest selling operating system which is not tied to a specific computer hardware manufacturer or supplier, and is available for micro, mini and mainframe computers. UNIX occupies the position in the minicomputer and mainframe world that is currently held by MS/PC-DOS in the PC world.

There are perhaps a dozen other successful non-proprietary operating systems on sale in the field; none yet challenges UNIX in terms of sales, let alone in terms of availability of hardware and software. This book does not attempt to compare these operating systems, as this would take considerable amounts of necessarily subjective technical detail, but a comparison with Pick is to be found in Chapter 8 to provide background on another popular non-proprietary operating system.

Being ahead of others in sales is not necessarily a recommendation unless the individual purchaser can see cogent reasons for choosing one operating system over another. Here the background of increasing acceptability of UNIX to users indicates the capability of satisfying requirements; more people are buying UNIX because it can do what they want.

Although recognising the success, viability and quality of many UNIX implementations, there are very few operating systems that really achieve good quality communication between man and machine, and much further work remains to be done to improve the situation. However, UNIX is the important operating system in the current environment, and seems likely to remain dominant for many years, given the investment of time and resources of so many able manufacturers and suppliers.

INDEPENDENCE

UNIX is not controlled by a single vendor or sold from a single point; many suppliers offer versions or types of products based upon or looking like UNIX. In fact, it is becoming difficult to identify a minicomputer or mainframe supplier who does not offer UNIX. Therefore the customer is not linked into a single manufacturer's hardware product range, and can also select suitable software from a large range of products.

One of the current problems worrying many suppliers of UNIX-like products is that AT&T, the original producers of UNIX, have entered into a partnership with Sun Microsystems, who are a supplier of UNIX products. This partnership is seen by many other suppliers as providing an unfair advantage to Sun, to the detriment of other suppliers, as Sun will have access to new developments before anyone else. To contain this situation, an organisation called the Open Software Foundation has been created by these discontented suppliers, which is concentrating on AIX, the flavour of UNIX supplied by IBM. Further detail on this situation can be found in Chapter 4 Standards and UNIX.

Many software houses have designed software to run under UNIX, as it is easy to convert software from one UNIX version to another, or 'port' across from one machine to another, so that a package written for one machine can be used on another. Therefore the user can select components for a system from a range of suppliers, with a high degree of probability that the system will function satisfactorily as a whole.

STANDARDS

Although there is as yet no single UNIX standard, the vast amount of effort being put into achieving a standards superstructure indicates the willingness of users and suppliers to work together to produce workable compliance between differing implementations. Hopefully, this will lead towards full standards status soon; in any case it seems that the market wants agreed unification and this wish is conditioning suppliers' attitudes.

There are currently three major standards initiatives: UNIX System V Interface Definition (SVID) from AT&T; Posix from the X/Open group; and AIX which is being promoted by the Open Software Foundation. It is very difficult to define points of difference between these initiatives, and it is important to note that none has yet become an international standard. SVID can be considered to be a *de facto* standard, but does not dominate the market. Greater detail on standards can be found in Chapter 4.

UNIX FEATURES

UNIX is a multi-tasking, multi-user system, so a single processor unit can be used by a number of users at terminals, and each user can run several tasks simultaneously. UNIX is a general-purpose operating system which can tackle most types of use; it is not (as is often stated) just an educationalist's toy, but is as easily capable of handling office, industrial and scientific usage. The majority of British universities employ UNIX systems for training and teaching, so there are many graduates leaving universities each year who have UNIX experience.

It is relatively easy to learn to use as there are comparatively few commands and fairly straightforward syntax. On the other hand it is easy to protect naive users from the system by option menus and good-quality application software. UNIX is not particularly user-friendly — few good operating systems are — but essentially it should be left to the application programs to provide the user interface.

There are many proprietary and non-proprietary multi-user operating systems; Pick, BOS and UNIX are the leading non-proprietary systems but UNIX is far ahead in terms of availability over a range of hardware and also in terms of availability of software packages.

Range of Hardware

UNIX is available from many sources and runs on a vast range of sizes and types of hardware. It is possible to start with a pilot study supporting half-a-dozen user terminals and grow the system to support thousands of users, mixing hardware makes and connecting together complex networks.

As UNIX is available on so many different machines, from personal computers to Cray supercomputers, it becomes possible for software houses to enhance profits by writing software on one make of hardware and then transferring programs to other makes.

A viewpoint specifically mentioned by many of the user organisations interviewed for this book is that it is easy for users to make the transition from personal computers (PCs) to UNIX-based systems because:

- it is possible to select from a range of different suppliers and compare like with like;

- software can be purchased 'off-the-shelf' and demonstrated before purchase;

- other sites using similar systems can be visited;

- software prices are comparable with PC products on a 'per user' basis.

Range of Software

There is a vast and steadily increasing range of applications and specialist programs for UNIX systems, so it is possible to buy programs already written to suit a particular trade or profession, that will run on a variety of different hardware systems.

It becomes possible for users to protect investment in software because UNIX packages can be transferred to another machine. A range of good development tools also speed development of in-house systems.

High-quality database systems can set aside the need for writing an application system by providing a user-friendly framework that is acceptable to untrained staff for normal day-to-day use.

Good Communications Facilities

Networking facilities are implicit in the design structure of UNIX; simple input/output device handling also makes for easy fitment of modems for further external connection to private or public telephone services.

This same ease of connection gives rise to worries about security as it can be easy for a hacker to gain access to a system. There is no easy answer to this problem as much depends on the nature and content of the system. NCC publish a number of books on data security (see Bibliography).

UNIX lends itself readily to use with communications equipment such as modems. Electronic mail and LANs are often features native to a UNIX implementation, and AT&T's UNIX V.3 kernel has Level 4 (transport layer) of the ISO Open Systems Interconnection (OSI) embedded in it.

Cost Effectiveness

Because UNIX hardware tends to be sold on a highly competitive basis, and with so many suppliers offering products giving equivalent performance, hardware prices are lower. In the software field, as a software house can recoup development costs over a much larger number of sales because the program will run on a much larger range of hardware, prices are also lower than for proprietary operating systems. Software prices are in fact comparable with products for PCs in terms of price per user.

Portability

A program can be written on one machine and transferred to another without great difficulty. A number of software products are available to further ease portability.

Expansion Capability

UNIX systems can be easily expanded by adding extra terminals and increasing disk storage. If necessary, much greater expansion can be achieved by linking further processors through a Local Area Network (LAN).

OTHER REASONS FOR CHOOSING UNIX

With so much activity from so many sources being directed towards UNIX, the market has accepted UNIX as a major force. The British government have asked that future systems conform to Posix, a standard evolved from UNIX, and the US government seem likely to adopt a similar position. In this situation, it is wise to look closely at the virtues of UNIX when considering purchase of a new system.

The advantages to the user of selecting UNIX also apply to the supplier, because it becomes easier to find linking products for systems; it is simpler to buy rather than to develop; it is easier to maintain an established product with many users because experience has developed in the use of the product. This means that hardware and software suppliers are pushing buyers towards UNIX-based systems, sometimes even at the expense of their own proprietary operating systems.

The remaining question, of course, is "Will UNIX be the system of the future? Or will it be AIX or Posix?". The question is essentially unanswerable, but the question does imply a solution. The operating system of the future will be either UNIX, Posix or AIX, or even some other UNIX-based product, but whatever it is, it will emerge from the UNIX world.

3   UNIX Features

WHAT IS UNIX?

UNIX is a multi-tasking, multi-user timesharing operating system which can be used on a wide range of hardware makes and sizes. The product was originally developed by AT&T, the American telecommunications giant. Versions of UNIX, or operating systems derived from UNIX, are also known under many other trade names, such as AIX (IBM), SINIX (Siemens), XENIX (for the IBM PC), UniCOS (for the Cray 2), Ultrix for DEC, and A/UX for the Apple Macintosh.

UNIX performs a similar range of functions as any other operating system. It acts as a link between the user, the operator and the machine. The operating system converts the assembly of electronic components that form a computer into a responsive system that can exhibit a low kind of intelligence. The operating system oversees communication between the processor and peripherals such as printers and external storage.

A rather artificial distinction has been made here between 'user' and 'operator'. In this context, the user is seen as the person seated at a terminal who is endeavouring to use the computer for some actual business purpose (for example, to run the monthly accounts); the operator is the person providing the necessary functions to keep the computer running (for instance, by loading the required tape).

The operating system is purely software, although it may be held in Read-Only Memory (ROM) chips as on some micros; UNIX is rather too large for economic storage in ROM and will normally be held on a magnetic disk. UNIX is loaded into the machine immediately after switching-on, generally automatically but occasionally by the operator using a specific series of simple instructions.

Instructions from the user or operator are typed on a keyboard and passed from the terminal to the main processor, where the instruction content is either intercepted by the program that is currently running or, when no program is running, taken by UNIX and interpreted as an operating system command. As UNIX is a multi-tasking operating system, each user can have several tasks running concurrently, so a command key on the terminal keyboard is dedicated to a function that will break back to UNIX without interrupting current programs. This enables the user to start new processes or close existing ones.

When a command is taken by UNIX, part of the operating system, called the "command interpreter", examines the typed characters. If the command interpreter finds that the typed input starts with characters that are identical to an instruction that is contained in the command set, the rest of the input is analysed for parameters to fit with that instruction. If the total command is valid, it is passed on for execution; if not, an appropriate error message will be selected from the library and sent back to the originator of the faulty command.

UNIX is interactive; when a user operates a terminal, the keystrokes communicate directly with the UNIX shell, which executes the commands. Commands can be strung together to generate short-cuts and extra utilities can easily be added into the system.

MAJOR FEATURES OF UNIX

The major features of UNIX are:

- large utility program set
- multi-user
- timesharing
- multi-tasking
- hierarchical file structure
- communications using 'pipes'
- device-independent system calls
- transparent process management
- easily extendable

Each of these features represents part of an interdependent whole, and as each feature has overlapping characteristics and is driven from, or called by, other parts of the system, it is not worthwhile to select a list in order of importance.

Large Utility Program Set

The system utilities have extended the facilities of UNIX very considerably. The user can add to the system and even set up methods of access varying with the terminal used, so that some terminal users can never access UNIX, only using the applications programs appropriate to their needs.

UNIX consists of two major components, the kernel and the utility program set. The utility program set consists of the system utilities. Both the kernel and the utility set are vital and integral parts of any UNIX implementation, and the basic system will always contain both.

Kernel

The kernel is the internal component of the operating system that cannot be modified by the user. The kernel provides the necessary start-up instructions ('booting') and also acts as the linkage between the system utilities and the hardware. The kernel schedules tasks and also manages the internal storage. Generally the kernel is written in C, but a small part is written in machine-specified assembly language. Porting to another machine can be done by writing a C code generator to adapt the kernel.

Some systems run UNIX as a process within another operating system and here the kernel is said to be 'hosted' under the main operating system.

Utility Program Set

There are currently over 200 utility programs in any version of UNIX, which form an absolutely integral part of the operating system. These routines and programs did not come from AT&T necessarily, but have been accreted from many sources, both commercial and educational. System utilities are generated using groups of UNIX operating system instructions, or C code. It is relatively easy for users to create new utilities using existing utilities to generate and test code.

The utilities perform such functions as file copying, directory listing and editing. The single most important utility is the shell, which acts as the interface between the user and the kernel, and is both command interpreter and also the programming language for generating new utilities.

There are two main types of shell in use: the Bourne Shell which is normally supplied with AT&T's UNIX, and the C-Shell which is based on products derived from the University of California at Berkeley. The shell provides commands, the linking of commands and the pipe facility, but it tends to be somewhat difficult for new users, so that many systems have overlaid the shell with a more friendly front end system.

The shell locates and loads programs from memory and executes them, and also operates series of commands called 'pipes'.

System utilities found in UNIX include text and file editing, electronic mail, formatting, assemblers, BASIC language interpreter, compilers and typesetting.

Multi-user

The system permits more than a single user to access the system at any one time, so that several programs and several sets of data can be simultaneously in use. UNIX also prevents any one user blocking out everyone else by allocating each user 'time slices' (Figure 2.1) of the operation of the computer's processor; operation of one user's process is interrupted after the time slice, and every other user's time slice is processed before returning to the first user. This technique is called 'time sharing'.

Timesharing

Every process that is running on the machine is run in a stream of processes that are executed in a series of steps, each step for one process separated in time from the next step by execution of steps for each of the other processes. This means that no one user can exploit the machine for a single process; everybody gets the same share of machine time.

Timeslicing is the normal technique employed during operation. However, it is possible to set up a series of priority users who may access more than their fair share of the system's facilities as required, and 'out of turn'.

Although normally each user will have a terminal and keyboard, and is connected to a

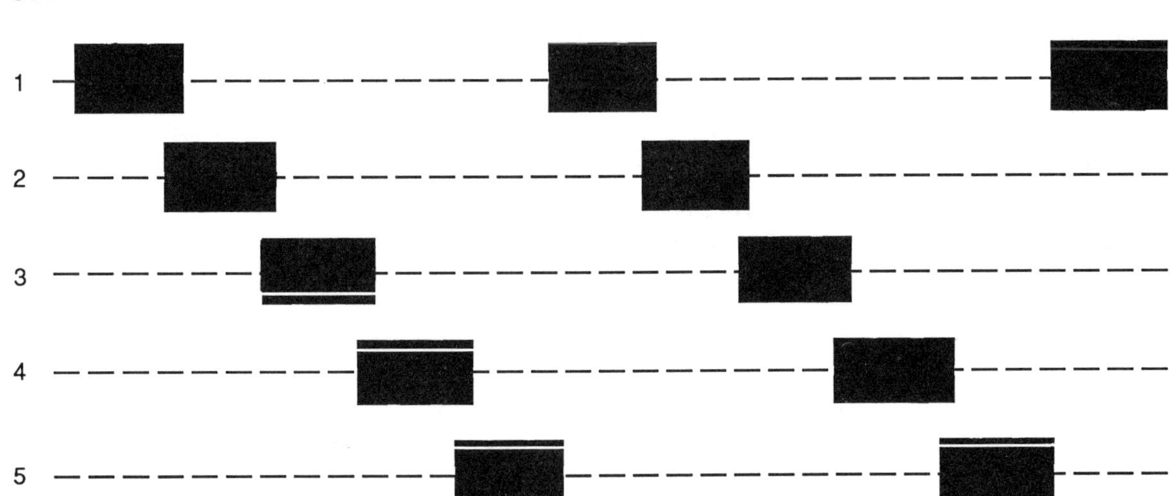

Figure 2.1   Time Slices

UNIX system by a serial communications line, UNIX provides excellent facilities for connection of remote terminals by modems, or by both Local Area Networks and Wide Area Networks.

Multi-tasking

Multi-tasking is the ability of a system to permit one user to run several tasks simultaneously. As a corollary to multi-user use, each of many users may be using the same program and the same data. Obviously this will require proper data protection by the operating system, otherwise the data will be overwritten and corrupted. The majority of major mainframe operating systems are multi-user, multi-tasking and time-sharing. The features of such a system are so useful that the vast majority of professional computer systems of all sizes above the homely PC now use similar operating systems.

Hierarchical File Structure

The storage of data on the UNIX system simply takes all input data for one file and stores it as a continuous string of bytes, without consideration of whether the data is numerical or alphabetic. An identical file format is used for programs, data and text. All buffering and storing of data is not visible to the user; the system takes care of these facilities and all file manipulation and protection in a transparent way so that naive users do not need to understand the operations.

Files within UNIX are held in a hierarchical structure, so that each file is held within a directory, which may itself be a part of a superior directory. (Directory structure is shown in Figure 2.2.) Each file has a name, and is found by referring to the file name within its directory. This forms what is termed the path name which is built up from the directory and file name separated by a slash character '/'. Thus an actual file name might be:

/unix/new/test/rab/file1

where the file 'file1' is found in directory 'rab', which is located in superior directory 'test', which is a sub-directory of 'new', which is a sub-directory of 'unix'. As this is a somewhat cumbrous name for a file, UNIX uses the technique of a current working directory for each

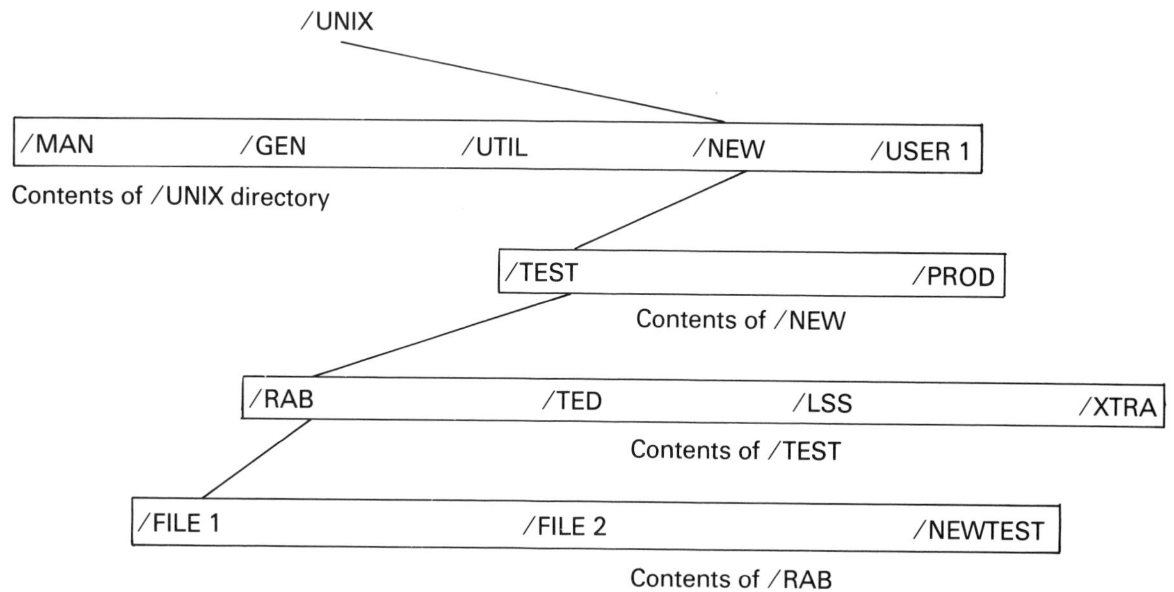

Figure 2.2   Directory Structure

user, where files can be referred to by only those parts of the name below the current directory, so in 'test' directory, '/rab/file1' would find the file 'file1'.

Obviously, many different files can exist in the complete system with the same file name; the files must be found using the correct path names so a file name must be unique within the directory.

Multi-user systems must protect files from accidental or deliberate corruption by unauthorised users. This is done in UNIX by using three types of file access and three types of user. As peripherals such as printers and terminals are also accessed by means of device files, this provides a method for determining the type of a peripheral and controlling it.

File access types are:

- read
- write
- execute

File users are classified as the:

- owner
- users in the same group
- all others

Any file can be set to provide one type of access to one type of user — so that a particular file may be set up as *read* to all *group* members, or *execute* to *all users*, or *write* to only the *owner*. Users in the same group would tend to share the same directories and therefore have access to the same range of files.

The byte stream file format also applies to directories and furthermore each terminal is connected by using a special file called a *device file* so that the same range of access types and user types even applies to each terminal.

Communications Using 'Pipes'

A pipe is a connection between two UNIX processes. Using the simple file structure, it is easy to link from one file to another, or one process to another. The pipes retain the correct linkages so as to permit a user to quickly switch from one process to another. The pipe connects the output of one process to the input of another so that it is possible to string together commands dealing with files to complete a whole range of file operations.

'Piping' of processes allows the user very considerable power over the operation of the machine in terms of allocating output resources and setting up terminal use. The facility is one of the reasons that skilled operations staff may not be necessary on a simple system for handling the usual routine tasks, and it is often possible to dispense entirely with skilled system operators.

Device-independent System Calls

Because all files, even special device files such as terminals, are treated in a consistent manner and are held as byte streams, all calls to use parts of the system such as peripherals deal with all devices in the same way. Although this may appear to give problems, such as when attempting to read from a printer, the device file will have been issued with proper file access type and user type.

Transparent Process Management

The management of a UNIX system must provide control over creation and start-up of a process, the timesharing of this process with any others that are currently running, provision of system resources such as memory and peripherals, and linking with required files. All of these operations are conducted by UNIX in such a way as to be invisible to the user, so that no specialist knowledge is needed to understand what is happening.

A number of further operations also occur during the operation of a system with several processes running simultaneously. Again the user may remain unaware of these operations unless a failure occurs. For example, if there is insufficient memory to start a new process it may be necessary for the system to write a current process away on a disk temporarily, awaiting its turn of the memory. This would not normally impinge on the user.

Originally UNIX systems ran out of working memory rather quickly and were obliged to write programs and data away to disk quite often. This consumed disk space and tended to overload disk input/output procedures so that the system would be 'clogged up' with calls to and from disk. The situation could arise when so many input/output procedures were awaiting execution that nothing else could be done! Recent UNIX versions allocate memory in 'pages' so that if it is necessary to write processes away to disk then the amount of disk storage taken over is much reduced.

Easily Extendable

It is easy to add additional resources to the system up to its maximum capacity, at which point it may well be possible to continue extension by linking several systems into a network. Further, links to other systems can be transparent to the user. There are two types of system in common use that may well be encountered in system specifications: Network File System and Remote File System.

NETWORK FILE SYSTEM (NFS)

NFS is a distributed file system, providing users with transparent access to files that may be held on other computers in the same network. The remote files seem to the user to be part of his or her own file system, so there is no need to transfer files by copying across from one machine to another before use. NFS is in fact a *de facto* standard, originally put together by Sun MicroSystems, and issued as source code in public domain software.

NFS was available under the Berkeley 4.2 BSD version of UNIX, and there is a release under UNIX System V, licensed by the Instruction Set in Europe. NFS can be implemented as a single way system on non-UNIX machines to provide access to UNIX files without providing access to the non-UNIX machine's files.

Users can share NFS files across the whole network without needing local copies so that storage volumes can be kept at a reasonable level. It may be feasible to dedicate a machine as a file server to reduce data flow and exploit higher performance drives on this machine, which may also help to cut the cost of future additional workstations as they will not require so much storage.

NFS also permits a single version of an application program to be used, reducing the problems of different versions in use by several users, and permits the use of a single version of particular application files, so ensuring that anyone is using the same data.

NFS access to files is controlled to protect files, and files must be made accessible to remote users by local action on the first occasion, and then by use of a remote 'mount' command.

REMOTE FILE SHARING (RFS)

RFS is AT&T's distributed file system, originally released as part of UNIX System V release 3.0. RFS gives remote access to all files, with pipes and access to special device files, but also supports full record and file locking. This makes files available for much greater use, and a greater spread of file use throughout the network, but machines in the network will have to exhibit greater compatibility at the binary level. RFS gives access to files throughout the system as if they were files on the user's own machine.

RFS allows suitably qualified users to easily access any appropriate files from any terminal, remote or local. RFS also will simplify systems administration as the systems administrator can access all files and control the complete system, no matter how many processors are linked.

The major difference between NFS and RFS is that NFS can support non-UNIX applications.

4   Standards and UNIX

INTRODUCTION

Standards are vital in industry to ensure that the customer gets good and reliable products; to make it easier to design and manufacture products; to simplify communications between products; and to ease transition from one product to another. Standards are important in terms of safety for the user, for the home and for the environment.

Where the standard is an operating system spread over the whole computer industry, the benefits should be very considerable. Firstly, software packages are not restricted to a single manufacturer's range of hardware, so that more packages will be available to the buyer for a particular machine. This also means that the user is not tied to a specific hardware supplier. Investment in a particular software package will be retained even if the hardware is changed, and data files will not need recreation on upgrading to another machine. Links can be established between machines to share files and application programs. Finally, users' knowledge of the system is not lost when the organisation buys other hardware.

In the past, some manufacturers were not keen on promoting standards as they wished to tie users to the manufacturers' own product ranges. However, hardware suppliers are now more aware of the high prime cost of software development and are more willing to let others provide the software. As software writers need a volume market to repay the development costs, they try to make a new package fit as many types of hardware as possible; this is made much easier if there is a common denominator, such as a standard operating system, covering a range of different hardware manufacturers. Thus, a standard operating system is good for both hardware and software suppliers, as well as providing benefits to users.

STANDARDS BODIES

There are a considerable number of both national and international standards bodies with an interest in UNIX (see Table 4.1). In the UK, the British Standards Institute (BSI) is the national body, which can prepare national standards and also consider proposed international standards. BSI is an independent body, with technical committees containing members from government, manufacturers, users and professional bodies. It is supported by voluntary contributions from industry and a contribution from central government. BSI has a working panel on Posix, IST/5/15, a technical subcommittee of IST/5 (Programming Languages).

In the US, much work for UNIX has been done by the Institute for Electrical and Electronic Engineers (IEEE) (often pronounced as 'eye-triple E'). All standards from this

ANSI	American, national
BSI	British, national
CEN	European
CEPT	European
CENELEC	European
CCITT	International
DIN	German, national
ECMA	European
IEC	International
ISO	International

Table 4.1   Standards Bodies Important to UNIX

body carry the IEEE prefix. ANSI is the American National Standards Institute and performs a similar role to BSI. The National Bureau of Standards (NBS) has produced a Federal Information Processing Standard (FIPS), constituting the procurement policy of the US Federal Government, which relates to draft 12 of IEEE P1003.1. The NBS has also produced the PCTS-Posix Conformance Test Suite, based on AT&T's SVVS subset. NBS has produced an Applications Portability Profile which gives a list of FIPS covering the operating system environment; this should permit applications programs to be portable at the source code level.

There are various European standards bodies with importance for the computer industry: Comité Européen De Normalisation (CEN) (for general standards), Conférence Européenne des Administrations des Postes et Télécommunications (CEPT) (for post and telecommunications standards); and Comité Européen Electrique (CENELEC) (for electrical, electronic and information technology).

The Commission for the European Community (CEC) is responsible for the harmonisation of standards activity throughout the European Community. The Public Procurement Subcommittee-Information Technology (PPSC-IT) is made up of representatives of purchasing agencies from European states, such as CCTA from the UK. PPSC-IT will receive the CEC project report 'Which UNIX for GPOS' (GPOS is the General Portable Operating System defined by ITUSA — see later).

A further European standards body is the European Computer Manufacturers Association (ECMA). Users are not represented on ECMA, but this body has a good record of effective liaison with ISO, ANSI and IEEE in establishing technical content of many recent computer standards.

The international standards authority covering computers and computing is the International Standards Organisation (ISO). Most national standards bodies are represented as members within ISO. ISO standards carry the letters ISO plus a four-digit number; sometimes also ISO/DIS (draft international standards) for proposed standards at an advanced stage, and ISO/DP for draft proposals. Again, there is UK representation in ISO.

ISO Technical Committee 97 (TC97) are responsible for information processing standards. Subcommittee 22 (SC22) consider programming languages and SC21 consider Open Systems Interconnection. A Special Working Group of SC22 are considering System Software Interface (SSI) which will probably include Posix definition, and Working Group 5

(WG5) of SC21 are looking at Operating System Command and Response Language (OSCRL) which is an attempt to define a human interface to a standard operating system. ISO will be voting on Posix as a draft international standard in October 1988.

In the telecommunications field the international body is CCITT (Comité Consultatif International Télégraphique et Téléphonique, an agency of the United Nations). The International Electrotechnical Commission (IEC) interests itself in electrical (as opposed to electronic) standards-making, but has done considerable valuable work on computers and office equipment, especially in terms of safety. CCITT, CCIR and IEC liaise with ISO, rather than being members.

Standards bodies are normally made up from users and manufacturers, but technical standards in computing, telecommunications and information technology tend to run ahead of user needs and are often proposed by individual manufacturers or groups of manufacturers. User groups are often represented on major committees.

USER GROUPS

Several user groups have appeared in the UNIX arena because AT&T made it clear that external groups could have considerable impact on the development of UNIX. Many universities in the States have had influence, especially the University of California at Berkeley. User groups quickly sprang up in the US, and as UNIX became important in the UK, similar organisations appeared in Britain, the major ones being /usr/group/UK, ITUSA and the European UNIX User Group (EUUG).

/usr/group are a US trade association who have put a great deal into the IEEE standards work, especially the P1003 committees. Technical working groups still are defining further topics for future work, including graphics, distributed file systems, networking, security and transaction processing.

/usr/group/UK are the UK equivalent of the /usr/group, the UNIX user group in the USA. /usr/group/UK has over 600 members, with about 50% being suppliers and software houses. ITUSA is the Information Technology Users Standards Association, which was formed to encourage users to participate in standards-making activities, and also publishes information to permit standards to be more widely used. ITUSA has identified a list of UNIX features required by users and has termed this the General Portable Operating System (GPOS). ITUSA will endorse Posix.

X/OPEN

X/Open, founded in 1984, is a group of competing manufacturers with the common aim of developing and marketing systems which conform to agreed standards. Members are Bull, DEC, Ericsson, Fujitsu, Hewlett-Packard, ICL, AT&T, Nixdorf, NCR, Nokia, Olivetti, Philips, Siemens, Sun and Unisys. IBM has expressed some interest in joining, and at the time of writing had just applied for entry, and is represented on the US IEEE Posix committee. X/Open has generally concentrated on development of interfaces to UNIX, and has produced standards for C and other high-level programming languages, but is now committed to the development of a common application environment (CAE). CAE is based on UNIX System V Interface Definition (SVID), and has been endorsed by American standards bodies. X/Open has published a 'Portability Guide' which describes the CAE.

X/Open has produced a specification called XVS (X/Open System V Specification) which is closely based on SVID with annotations to define interfaces and options within interfaces which are not completely portable between current versions from various suppliers. X/Open intend to support Posix and are working with IEEE to achieve convergence between Posix and their own definition of System V.

XVS forms only a part of the X/Open Portability Guide. Other sections cover the development of applications which work in different languages; ISAM (Indexed Sequential

Access Method) file structures from Informix Corporation's C-ISAM Version 2.10; and SQL (Structured Query Language) based on ANS X3.135-1986. The Guide contains a definition for 80-track floppy disks and half-inch magnetic tapes for inter-machine transfers. Standards are identified for C, Cobol, Pascal and Fortran. A vital part of the Guide recognises that, while UNIX was based on the ASCII seven-bit character set, European languages require eight-bit character sets to represent all the characters used in the languages, and Chinese and Japanese need 16-bit character sets.

It is important to remember that neither X/Open or IEEE are international standards organisations, and that conflicting motives exist within these groups for the nature and content of standards proposals. X/Open have been very active in the standards scene and are represented in IEEE P1003 (see Posix later). There has been discussion about merging X/Open's CAE and APP from the NBS.

CUE (COMMON UNIX ENVIRONMENT)

A new group of UK UNIX companies have formed themselves into the Common UNIX Environment (CUE), and are represented on X/Open technical committee meetings. The group (composed of both hardware and software companies) comprises: Bleasdale Computer Systems, Unisoft, The Instruction Set, Gartner ITL, Ferranti Computer Systems, Integrated Micro Products, benchMark Technologies, Cambridge Microcomputers and Lynwood. CUE aims are to demonstrate that UNIX standards work; to exchange technology among members; and to provide access to the international groups such as X/Open.

SIGMA

In Japan MITI (Ministry of International Trade and Industry) has sponsored a project known as SIGMA, which includes most major Japanese computer companies. This project is intended to perform a similar role to X/Open, and has already developed specifications for workstations, and is currently working on definitions for hardware and software interfaces for 32-bit computers.

DE FACTO STANDARDS

All the above organisations produce, or assist in producing, *official* standards. However, often the situation is complicated by the so-called *de facto* standards, which are not necessarily the output from a standards body, but have become so widespread as to represent the reality of the situation. An example here is the IBM-PC, often described as the industry standard. X/Open are prepared to incorporate international standards where they exist and to adopt *de facto* standards where no international standard applies.

STANDARDS AND UNIX

There are so many compatible and incompatible operating systems based on or using UNIX 'look and feel' that it is wrong to speak in most cases of UNIX versions, as this does not accurately reflect the relationship of a manufacturer's implementation of a UNIX-like system to AT&T's UNIX; instead the word 'flavour' has come into use.

There are various flavours of UNIX that have culminated in *de facto* but temporary standards; for example, AT&T developed a standard known as System V Interface Definition (SVID) that was a great step towards establishing a standard front end.

SYSTEM V INTERFACE DEFINITION (SVID)

SVID was intended to provide a definition of the external interface in terms of services provided by all System V systems. This includes the way the system appears to an application program, but does not lay down how the operating system performs these functions. This is termed the Base System. Extensions to the Base System are defined as additional services such as networking within 'Extensions to the Base System'. The final task of SVID was to define all external interfaces so that conforming applications will perform as defined within System V; this means that application programs can be completely portable across all System V implementations.

SVID is a definition of AT&T's UNIX, so that a number of BSD functions are not included, and also there is no definition of functions such as database management and enquiry systems. There is no mention of data layout on tape or floppy disk. However, the inclusion by AT&T of sections entitled 'Future Directions' does provide interesting predictions as to future extensions for graphics and interfaces, for example.

At this point it should be noted that UNIX is a trademark of AT&T and therefore only AT&T (and companies such as Olivetti who use AT&T's product) can claim to have machines running UNIX System V. Other manufacturers should use a different name unless they are full UNIX licence holders. For example DEC offers Ultrix and IBM AIX, both of which are SVID compatible. XENIX is also SVID compatible.

System V competed with Berkeley's 4.2. The current AT&T V.3 includes all of the Berkeley 'bells and whistles' so it seems that AT&T can appreciate good items (and fit them into their next version!), and this openness about system developments is one of the great strengths of UNIX.

POSIX (PORTABLE OPERATING SYSTEM INTERFACE FOR COMPUTER ENVIRONMENTS)

The American user group /usr/group wished to define a standard that would make UNIX truly machine portable, and as SVID was controlled strictly by AT&T, they wished to create greater independence. The /usr/group standard was based on System V, but sidestepped incorporation of BSD4.3 and XENIX features, and left no room for already established developments of System V. The standards committee then merged with the P1003 committee of the Institution of Electrical and Electronic Engineers (IEEE). As the volume of work necessary for the creation of a complete interface standard became apparent, P1003 split into subcommittees.

Subcommittee P1003.1, was given the task of preparing a Portable Operating System Interface for Computer Environments (POSIX) covering a programming language interface that can be used on many different systems for the applications interface. Subcommittee P1003.2 dealt with the shell and tools covering the user interface, P1003.3 verification and testing methodology, and P1003.4 covering real-time operation. The P1003.1 trial use standard, which was approved in 1986, gained over 75% approval, and is gaining commercial acceptance. It is intended that Posix will be approved for full use during 1988 and will then be submitted as a draft International Standards Organisation (ISO) standard.

Further subcommittees are working on real-time extensions (P1003.4), ADA bindings for Posix (P1003.5), and security extensions (P1003.6). Other topics to be tackled include: data management facilities, networking facilities, distributed systems facilities, graphics, parallel processing, high reliability facilities and the user interface.

Posix was conceived as an interface for a common operating system and has been pushed through towards an international standard in an amazingly short time. Posix was endorsed by 58 major manufacturers, including IBM and AT&T at the Uniforum UNIX conference in Washington DC during January 1987. ANSI seem likely to endorse Posix as an American standard, and it is likely that ISO will accept Posix as an application layer standard within the OSI (Open Systems Interconnection) model. ANSI have produced a specification for C, from the X3J11 committee, that has been circulated amongst UK software houses in draft form. The X3J11 committee has collaborated with the IEEE P1003.1 (Posix) committee. Standardisation of C will improve its reliability and portability. This in turn will make it easier to sell C worldwide.

Posix is based on AT&T's System V Interface Definition (SVID), and also incorporates features from Berkeley 4.2 and 4.3. It seems likely that ultimately UNIX will be replaced by

Posix. Again, as with SVID, Posix is a definition of an interface; there is no attempt to define the nature of the operating system so that any operating system which conforms to Posix rules can tender where Posix is required, even if its structure is totally different to UNIX. Posix effectively sits between an operating system and the application programs. There are minimal differences between Posix and SVID, but it is completely feasible for DEC to have a Posix-conformable operating system (Ultrix) which is not UNIX compatible.

The UK Government have endorsed UNIX by the adoption of the Posix interface and the X/Open portability guide. UK Government departments will buy over 200,000 workstations before 1992 and a significant proportion of these workstations will use UNIX. The Central Computer and Telecommunications Agency (CCTA), who provide a purchasing protocol for government departments, have instituted a system that requires all suppliers to conform to Posix. One of CCTA's main reasons for demanding UNIX is the cost and difficulty of converting software in government when current obsolete hardware is replaced; it has cost £3 million and 250 man-years for a government department to convert a personnel/payroll system from one operating environment from another, and this was on two sets of hardware from the same manufacturer.

THE OPEN SOFTWARE FOUNDATION (OSF)

A new and vitally important aspect of the UNIX world is the launch of the Open Software Foundation (OSF). The Foundation is to some extent the reaction to AT&T's activities, especially in terms of the relationship between AT&T and Sun.

AT&T is a vast company, with thousands of employees working on hundreds of different projects, only a few of which have any relationship with UNIX. This isolation complicates the exploitation of UNIX, which cannot be considered as a front-line product for a major telecommunications hardware manufacturer. So AT&T have been considering setting up a separate company for developing UNIX; also because the recent alliance with Sun Microsystems has caused widespread protests from users and other manufacturers that UNIX will now become a closed development project, with Sun dominating all changes. Certainly a major rewrite is planned by AT&T/Sun which will be written in a new version of the C programming language. A number of major members of X/Open threatened to bring legal actions against AT&T because Sun will be receiving an unfair advantage by means of its close links with AT&T; setting up a separate development company would sidestep this criticism.

Sun Microsystems have developed a chip series known as SPARC (Scaleable Processor Architecture) that is intended to exploit the great power of modern silicon chips for driving an operating system. These chips are Reduced Instruction Set Computing (RISC) technology that yields higher processing speeds. Sun are creating a range of machines built around these chips. AT&T and Sun are said to be developing future versions of UNIX specifically around these chip sets. This will mean that anyone wishing to use the latest version of UNIX will have to also use the SPARC chip set.

AT&T and Sun have developed a product for version 4 of System V which will give a front end with both windows and icons to provide a highly user-friendly interface; the product is called 'Open Look'. Open Look was developed using windowing technology from Xerox. AT&T claim that both Open Look and UNIX System V version 4 conform to X/Open and Posix standards. The press have dubbed this interface 'SPARCintosh' as it resembles in format Apple's Macintosh front-end. This is an indirect result of work done by Xerox on the human interface conducted at the Palo Alto Research Centre (PARC) from 1968 — work that previously spurred the development of the Apple Macintosh.

ICL are aligned with Sun/AT&T on the SPARC project, and remain committed to UNIX System V for the current product range. Xerox and Unisys have also made public statements expressing their commitment to SPARC.

In April/May of 1988 the situation reached a head and a group of companies with UNIX-based systems formed the Open Software Foundation (OSF) to develop an industry standard software environment based around a UNIX-like operating system. OSF members in June 1988 were IBM, DEC, Hewlett-Packard, Apollo, Siemens, Nixdorf and Bull. AT&T apparently refused an invitation to join, preferring to concentrate on making UNIX System V the industry standard, and indeed a further proposed standard is not helpful to users. It is, however, a considerable boost to UNIX to be promoted by such a powerful group of manufacturers.

The objectives of OSF are to develop, publish and distribute a standard operating system, which will be independent of a single supplier. It is assumed that this operating system will be UNIX-like, as it has been declared that it will be based on the IBM UNIX flavour, AIX. OSF will also develop subsystems such as database formats and communications interfaces to run within or link to the operating system. OSF will establish compliance testing procedures, and develop methods by which the standard can be developed. There will be finance for research into developments, and the Federation will develop distribution systems which will be independent of hardware suppliers.

OSF will define an Application Environment Specification (AES) which will make it easier to create portable applications. Interfaces will support Posix, X/Open and the NBS's APP specifications, so as to give applications portability at the source code level.

OSF members have each paid $12.8 million into a fund to start up, giving a total funding of $90 million to finance the project over three years. AIX, the UNIX flavour used by IBM, will form the basis of products which will be licensed to users and manufacturers. Membership of OSF is open to anyone, with costs to profit makers of $25,000 and non-profit making organisations paying $5000. The first products planned for release are the publication of the Posix interface and the X-Windows presentation system, but industry estimates are that it will take 18 months for OSF to prepare an actual operating system product that can compete with UNIX System V. Apollo's NCS has also been suggested as a future product. Member companies will also continue to develop and sell their own proprietary operating systems.

The initial product, 'Level 0 Applications Environment' is based on Posix. Future products will be based on AIX from IBM. The current list of contributions and sponsors is:

- Operating System (AIX) — IBM
- Tools for X-Windows — DEC
- Networking — Apollo
- National language support — Hewlett-Packard
- Multi-processor architecture — Groupe Bull
- Relational database — Relational Technology
- Relational database — Nixdorf
- Communications — Siemens

Over 200 other organisations including AT&T have been invited to join the OSF.

OTHER STANDARDS ACTIVITY

Many manufacturers are working hard at establishing effective standards, not necessarily their own, in order to push onwards with the development of a truly portable applications environment that will permit spread of applications software and permit suppliers to pick up on off-the-shelf packages. For example, the Instruction Set have been given the task of converging the Portability Guide and Posix, and IBM have secured the contract to develop the conformance testing suite for Posix. This work will be carried out by MINDCRAFT. Root developed the VSX product for X/Open, and UniSoft developed SVVS for AT&T. Root and Unisoft are represented on P1003.

Apollo Computer is trying to encourage users to make a *de facto* standard of the Apollo product NCS (Networking Computer System), which uses X-Windows. Apollo have waived the licence fee for NCS and have set up a standards forum. NCS is written in C and uses common networking protocols such as TCP/IP, Domain, DDS, IBM's SNA and MAP/TOP.

Altos, who have been suppliers of UNIX for a long time, have put together UNIX V/386, the first commercial fusion of UNIX and XENIX. V/386 is fully compatible with UNIX System V, with UNIX V Release 3, Santa Cruz Operation (SCO) and Microsoft's version. AT&T have a technology agreement with Altos, so UNIX V/386 will form the basis of the AT&T/Microsoft UNIX/XENIX product to be launched in autumn 1988.

AT&T's current version, System V.3 has remote file facilities, and the ability to link MS-DOS and UNIX applications, and permits the use of UNIX for a small workgroup to use PCs to link across to a UNIX departmental server using a LAN. The merged UNIX System V/Berkeley 4.2 from AT&T and Sun should be available in 1989.

However, the unification drives towards standardisation are resulting in a tiered environment, with Posix (P1003.1) in the centre, enclosed by AT&T's SVID and finally enclosed by X/Open's CAE. ITUSA have proposed a wider definition than CAE; this has not yet reached a proposed international standard status.

A vital part of any standardisation of UNIX is a properly constituted independent conformance testing organisation. IBM are developing a Posix conformance testing suite, but until a more settled international standard has emerged for UNIX it will be difficult to develop suitable test methodologies. It seems more likely that the Open Systems Foundation systems, together with Posix, will be the ultimate UNIX-based products.

In the UK, NCC have provided a conformance testing product under the aegis of a consortium of NCC, X/Open, British Telecom, and Computer Resources International (CRI). The project is entitled CTS-2 Posix (based on NBS's PCTS-Posix) and is funded by the European Commission to establish a harmonised European Test Service for Posix. The NCC will coordinate with the American National Bureau of Standards.

5 Implications of Using UNIX

INTRODUCTION

The implications of using or selecting UNIX are related to the features of the operating system as well as the features of any hardware system likely to be selected to run the operating system. The large range of machine sizes that can accept a version of UNIX, 'from 4 to 1,000 users', means that some of the initial sizing implications on hardware selection can be sidestepped, at least during the information-seeking phase of selection. However, the selection of UNIX should exploit the desirability of its good features, but it is vital to reveal and understand the bad points, where UNIX has features which are positively undesirable.

UNIX FEATURES

The features of UNIX that are often regarded as most significant by market commentators are that UNIX:

- is portable
- is flexible
- supports networking

This list will be contrasted later with users' views of UNIX success points, and suppliers' views.

Portability

Portability implies the ability to create a program on one machine and easily transfer it to another. UNIX makes it easy to move current programs to another machine even from another hardware manufacturer. This of course is because the operating system is written in a specific, portable language (C) and needs little work to adapt to another hardware environment.

Although portability is regarded by many suppliers and many journalists as a vitally important aspect of UNIX it will convey little benefit to a user who will rarely change machine type more often than every five years and who is unlikely to wish to transfer software on a regular basis. Portability will be of great benefit to organisations with many different types, makes and sizes of machine, not only in saving time in creation of new software but also because operation policy can be standardised throughout the organisation.

A survey by Commslogic, published in Informatics, December 1987, showed that only 33%

of users had attempted to port applications to UNIX — rather surprising in view of UNIX portability being one of the most commonly quoted benefits.

The great advantage of portability to all users is the ease with which package and proprietary software can be readily ported to other machines by suppliers, thus moving UNIX-based machines towards the situation on personal computers where suppliers prepare software to suit the dominant IBM *de facto* standard. Ultimately, this will result in an off-the-shelf buying situation, and proper like-with-like product comparisons will be feasible.

Flexibility

UNIX has proved itself capable of running almost any type of applications software, and working in almost every type of business. Flexibility is conferred by the simple file structures and transparent operation of UNIX.

The contrary view of flexibility is that the system is too simple, with many areas where insufficient data is given to properly monitor the system or control unauthorised access. The deficiencies can be met by carefully chosen software additions, and in fact such extensions are the commonest type of added software in the US.

Supports Networking

UNIX is capable of supporting extensive networks and providing easy access to files through the network. As organisations require more and better links between remote sites in order to provide more accurate management information, networks become more vital, and UNIX can be readily used in the networking role.

Until about three years ago, Berkeley-based implementations tended to have better networking qualities, using TCP/IP (Transmission Control Protocol and Internet Protocol) or XNS protocols which were both standard with BSD (Berkeley Standard Definition) 4.3. The current AT&T version, System V Release 3, supports the Streams architecture; TCP/IP and low cost versions of Ethernet are also now available. From 1987 onwards more companies have been providing communications packages with networking support for IBM's SNA (System Network Architecture) and a wide range of other manufacturers' protocols.

OTHER REASONS FOR BUYING UNIX

It is apparent when talking to users of UNIX systems that the commentators' views are not necessarily reflected by users of the system, and, in fact, the reason most commonly mentioned by users for buying a UNIX system is the independence from hardware suppliers. The vast range of software available was also very commonly regarded as an important feature.

A number of other reasons were expressed as important factors in making the selection of UNIX or UNIX-based systems. Few of these reasons relate to the type of hardware or its manufacturer. Instead the reasons for selection tend to confirm the maturity of the user base; where so many consultants have been saying for so long that the place to start is with the software, many UNIX users have done exactly that. They have found, and have had demonstrated, a suitable software package (or several) for their businesses that performs part of the requirement, and then later realised that the package runs under UNIX, which allows them much more freedom with hardware selection and gives access to a vast range of other software.

From users' views, expressed both during informal interviews and in a number of press articles published through 1987 and 1988, the list shown in Table 5.1 has been compiled. Again, it is not in any order of priority; different users had differing views on the importance of a particular aspect.

    * hardware independent
    * software range
    * non-pioneering
    * saves suppliers' development time and support
    * off-the-shelf applications
    * size range
    * good high-level language
    * office automation

Table 5.1   Important Factors in Choosing UNIX

Some of these points have been previously examined, or are self-explanatory. Non-pioneering refers to the situation that UNIX is an established 'standard' operating system with software of all types that is already in use; rarely will users find that their site is the test site for a new package, although of course if the program has been specifically written for that user then pioneering will be restricted to testing that program.

In the same way, the saving of time and support from suppliers is an advantage to users because it will reduce initial and running costs for program and maintenance. The range of good software development tools enables users to generate their own software, or use one of the excellent database systems to create a unique application.

The good high-level language referred to in the list above is C; some programmers regard C as a low-level language but the language permits fast development and supports structured organisation. Most other programming languages are available under UNIX, but C has been coming to the fore lately as more manufacturers put it onto their hardware. C is often referred to as a programmer's language, as it can work to nearly as low a level as an assembler language but without the poor productivity typical of assemblers (Kolodziej, 1988).

UNIX is chosen for office automation systems because it:

– is portable
– is easily extendable
– facilitates communications
– offers remote file systems
– offers PC links

Portability, already discussed, is obviously of great value in permitting the spread of a particular software system throughout an office network.

UNIX is easily expanded by adding further processors with additional terminals and linking through with a LAN. The Remote File Sharing (RFS) or Network File System (NFS) provides look-through facilities to files not held locally so as to make the multi-processor system as transparent to the user as possible.

Electronic mail and also external communications links are regarded as the hallmark of UNIX systems, and certainly there are a profusion of support elements within UNIX for communications and a wealth of good software. LANs can be readily fitted to a UNIX system and as AT&T's UNIX V.3 Kernel has embedded Level 4 of the ISO 7-layer model (transport layer), UNIX communications are trending towards conformance to international standards. In addition, there are many packages for PCs running under MS-DOS or OS/2 to link to UNIX.

Two further points have emerged from talking to users who have converted from PCs. It was apparent that the performance of the PCs was disappointing for a number of reasons, including poor data security and the difficulty of disseminating up-to-date data. Although UNIX does not completely solve these problems, it can help a great deal. Users remarked on two specific features of UNIX systems that resemble PC systems: buying software off-the-shelf and the transparency of UNIX.

It is easy to buy software packages off-the-shelf for UNIX, and relatively easy to install new packages. As with PCs, this situation encourages purchase of new software that is likely to run on the machine without a long and costly period of installation by highly-skilled specialists. It can be as simple as loading in a floppy disk and typing half-a-dozen commands.

In fact, many aspects of using UNIX systems resemble the same activities on PCs and many commands are similar. UNIX systems do not present to users an operating system superstructure that is normally invisible and that requires skilled attention from specialists. This helps to ease the transition from a PC to the much more powerful UNIX environment.

Moving from a PC to UNIX environment is quite easy for most users and presents considerable advantages over the PC within the corporate environment. UNIX systems are based on hard-disk drive configurations and are not restricted by floppy disk size, and so there is little possibility of particular data being hidden away on someone's floppy disk. UNIX requires proper care and therefore will improve system discipline with regard to files, so that it is possible to overcome the previous situation where incomplete or outdated data could be used. However, the openness of files can give rise to fears about data security.

A number of manufacturers, including IBM, offer UNIX/XENIX on PCs. These implementations have not been particularly successful in terms of sales, possibly because many users have difficulty with existing single-user operating systems and will be presented with insuperable difficulties when faced with a multi-user, multi-tasking system. The much more powerful 80386 based systems will require better operating systems, so here UNIX/XENIX is likely to become a standard with today's more experienced PC user.

PC LINKS

The modern office has many PCs in use for a variety of roles; UNIX can provide supporting communications facilities so that it should be possible to use the PCs as terminals or workstations. These PCs may also need data files held on the UNIX machine for MS-DOS applications, and the simple communications links or RFS/NFS can ease retrieval and transfer.

Manufacturers have a natural interest in the reasons why users purchase their machines, and although the results from expensive market research investigations are rarely made public, Apricot have conducted a survey amongst purchasers of Apricot XENIX systems. Reasons are listed in Table 5.2.

Most of these points have been discussed earlier. Migration tools are methods to easily transfer software from one machine to another using the same operating system. These tools are available for UNIX and some other operating systems, and even for transfer from one operating system to another.

Protection of investment in software has become critical with the increasing cost of

* hardware independence
* ever increasing range of application software
* migration tools
* network connectivity strengths
* protection of investment
* distributed processing
* wide area communications

Table 5.2   Why End Users Choose UNIX (Source – Apricot)

program design and development. Maintenance of systems and continual amendment mean that it is essential to retain a software system for as long as possible. Incompatibility of hardware systems, even from the same manufacturer, meant in the past that great effort had to be made to convert software for use on a new system; UNIX can prevent this by giving the user the ability to quickly move software to another machine. Further, the software can be used over a range of different types of machine.

WORKSTATIONS

UNIX is not necessarily the best operating system for workstations; for example TRIPOS, a relatively obscure British system is probably nearer to users' real requirements for a desktop-sized machine. There are major differences: for example, UNIX is multi-user against TRIPOS single-user; UNIX uses the well-known C language against the little-known BCPL; UNIX is a virtual memory system whereas most versions of TRIPOS are real memory only. In spite of this, TRIPOS has scored successes: it forms the basis of AMIGADOS, the operating system for the Commodore Amiga; and it is in widespread use through British universities. TRIPOS uses only a fraction of the memory of UNIX (Mills 1987).

Against this, UNIX has no specific features favouring it over other operating systems but it is the leading non-proprietary system and in this situation it is unlikely that other systems, no matter what their features, will be widely accepted; it is much more likely that UNIX or UNIX flavours will take on some of the features found in the technically more suitable operating systems. This is certainly what happened with PC-DOS in the micro world; as so many systems were installed PC-DOS became the environment, and all new ideas were grafted on to PC-DOS.

Systems based on Sun's SPARC chips will bring much more power to the workstation, with a dependence on UNIX as the native system. In this situation, the office workstation can become far more than a terminal simply giving access to a range of software from the main organisational computer, and can effectively provide high levels of computing power locally. The current range of high power personal computers with the Intel 80386 chips are already capable of providing local computing as well as links to remote machines; the problem is the operating systems currently in use.

UNIX AND MANUFACTURERS

Taking on UNIX as the standard operating system for a hardware supplier conveys many benefits. For example, Apricot, the UK micro manufacturer, selected XENIX because it provided an operating system that can support from 1 to 1000 users. Starting with from 1 to 4 users on the 286 XEN-i, up to 8 on the 386 XEN-i, up to 32 on the 386 Tower or the 386 VX, and reaching up to 1000 users on the VX9000 series parallel processors.

System software support is also easier for Apricot on one operating system, and there are good products and support from AT&T, Microsoft, and Santa Cruz Operation (SCO), the XENIX supplier. Because Apricot have committed suppliers, who are large enough to still be in business in a few years time, Apricot can rely on development products coming along without committing large resources themselves.

Apricot can pick up on the large range of good software products from UNIX houses. Systems development tools such as compilers, and migration tools are readily available to speed development of quality software. High-quality presentation systems, fourth-generation languages, and databases can permit the user to create specific applications software. A further range of software will come from migrating from MS-DOS packages.

Apricot are dedicated to achieving Open Systems Interconnection (OSI), and UNIX does not obstruct this drive; in fact it enhances it. Other points that favour the selection of UNIX are the availability of peripherals, especially communications components, such as modems and line drivers.

It has been suggested that one major computer supplier has lost \$4 billion in lost orders in the US and \$200 million in the UK as a result of not supporting Posix. Certainly the UK government wants Posix from suppliers, and although the operating system supplied by the major manufacturer is Posix conformable, most government contracts require 100% UNIX System V conformance. The supplier believes that in the current situation, the 'cosy' relationship between Sun and AT&T will mean that there will be two disparate types of UNIX; firstly, the Posix committee's type, implemented over a number of different manufacturers, and secondly the AT&T/Sun special version. In this situation, the supplier feels that his products will not be evaluated in a fair way.

This has been one of the major drives towards the formation of the Open Software Foundation.

UNIX AND SOFTWARE DEVELOPMENT

Integrated project support environments (IPSE) provide a framework in which software can be developed reliably. The European Esprit Programme has initiated a consortium of manufacturers comprising Bull, Olivetti, Siemens, Nixdorf, ICL and GEC, to produce an IPSE called PCTE (Portable Common Tool Environment). This could simplify the task of software development and reduce costs. PCTE may become a European standard, and as the proprietors are all members of X/Open, it seems natural to anticipate further product development through UNIX.

DISADVANTAGES OF UNIX

Aim Technology Survey

UNIX cannot be considered as a finalised product, although it has been in use and under development for nearly 20 years. Many features commonly found within or available for major mainframe operating systems are absent from the base versions. A survey by Aim Technology of UNIX users in the US found that the users believed that UNIX needed a number of improvements to meet their requirements (McKee, 1987). The proposed improvements are shown in Table 5.3.

> * System monitor
> * Back-up, archive and restore
> * Network monitor
> * Disk tuner
> * Job accounting
> * Job scheduler
> * Tape management

Table 5.3   User Suggestions for UNIX Improvements

System monitors collect and present data on system utilisation, permitting evaluation of total system capacity and daily usage. This can be important for multi-user operation in order to determine whether one user is obtaining an unfair slice of the machine, and monitoring is vital on complex networking systems. Job accounting complements the work of the system monitor in tracing use of system resources by users; UNIX notes log-on times for each user and timestamps each program with a 'when run' tag. User name and identifier, time of start and duration of run are generated and recorded but there are no specific utilities to analyse disk file usage.

Back-up facilities are not a point of high emphasis in UNIX systems; these activities are best performed manually, again a point of divergence from many mainframe systems. There are no inbuilt facilities for recording what file is on what disk or tape, and there are no automatic back-up, restore or archiving features. Disk tuning is the technique of assembling the files that have greatest use into an easily accessed area so as to speed up access. UNIX does not provide any system utilities for this function.

Job scheduling permits the scheduling of tasks to coincide with the availability of system resources; for example, so that the required printer is not printing something else when needed for a particular task. This is particularly important when dealing with files on disk, but again there is no specific job scheduling feature in UNIX. Although the time-sharing scheduler handles multiple tasks from terminal users, it can interrupt a transaction before completion, therefore artificially slowing down the whole system.

Tape management is important when maintaining data for several systems to be loaded at run time or for back-up, as there is no specific facility for keeping a tape content register by tape number. Many complex systems in the US have developed company-specific records systems which can be added to existing systems.

In addition to these features identified by Aim Technology, other problem areas are described below:

Transaction Processing

A major deficiency is the lack of provision for transaction processing. The file structure mitigates against on-line transaction processing because file structure is linked to the time-sharing concept. Files cannot be permanently attached to a particular job unless the application system can override the system's file control techniques. A package called Tuxedo provides some of the necessary facilities and has become popular in the USA.

There is an X/Open initiative on transaction processing for an international standard supported by the International Standards Organisation (ISO). Athough there was talk of enhanced transaction processing in the next UNIX System V release 4.0, this now looks unlikely.

User-friendliness

UNIX cannot be considered to be user-friendly, and early versions often responded with simple messages such as 'didn't work' or 'not found'. Some rather more brusque messages such as 'Can't you follow a simple instruction?' were also included. Commands are still short even to the point of terseness; for example, 'cp' copies files. It is rarely obvious what a command is intended to do. Although the short commands mean less typing, when considered with the 'wild-card' options, this can be dangerous; for example 'rm *' will erase all the files in the current directory without so much as a warning message.

The president of /usr/group (in USA) has said that an operating system need not be user-friendly, it should be up to applications programs to provide a 'front end' that provides a friendly interface to the user. Certainly it is often preferable in a system with many untrained users to protect users from the operating system so that all anticipated events can be handled by the user, especially if operation of the user system can be completely specified by a simple manual or built-in 'help' systems on the machine. This will reduce learning time and hopefully reduce the need for skilled support, although in this environment a 'help-desk' or information centre for end-users is an important part of a successful implementation.

IBM are advertising that they have put half-a-million extra lines of code into their AIX flavour of UNIX to make it more friendly. AIX is Posix conformable.

Graphics

Graphics has been an area where UNIX failed to shine compared with PC systems, but S-GKS is now certified for UNIX, and is written in C. Previously S-GKS has been available for VAX/VMS and MS-DOS. GKS (Graphics Kernel System) was the first international standard for graphics, and defines a standard library of tools and facilities for 2D graphics systems.

Windowing

Windowing is a technique of providing multi-tasking, so that one user can move from one task to another without having to close down each task before moving. Each task is held in a window, which can be brought up to the screen or set aside. In the PC world windowing is probably going to be more important than true multi-tasking as few PC tasks run for long periods without user attention and the majority of tasks are run in real time, not started and left running until the task is complete, such as when running a company payroll. On PCs interactive systems are the rule. Minicomputers, on the other hand, are commonly used for batch processing where the machine is set up with regular tasks — (such as payroll), which are run for a long and continuous period without user or operator intervention.

UNIX does not provide windowing within the base system, but Apollo Computer has a product called NCS (Networking Computer System), which uses X-Windows under UNIX. Apollo is likely to evolve a *de facto* standard of NCS, within the Open Software Foundation.

Machine Sizing

There are definite implications on machine sizing as any computer running UNIX needs a hard disk of at least 20 Mbytes and at least 1 Mbyte of RAM. UNIX ideally needs 500 Kb of RAM to start up. 512 Kb is probably the absolute minimum RAM size that could run UNIX. Most personal computers using the 8086 chip can run XENIX; micros based on 80286/80386 with memory management can run UNIX, as can 68000-based micros. The vast majority of suppliers of these machines can offer at least a proprietary version of UNIX, and will be offering products conforming to SVID-2 in 1988.

For example, the Apple version of UNIX, the A/UX system, will be loaded on to an 80Mb hard disk and the machine will be fitted with an additional 4Mb of RAM. A/UX encompasses AT&T's V2.2 and the Berkeley (BSD) versions 4.2 and 4.3. This will also allow the transfer of the approximately 3,000 Macintosh applications to A/UX. Apple have also made available a version of the Sun networking file system facilities. The recent link of DEC and Apple may mean further exploitation of Ultrix, DEC's UNIX flavour.

Data Security

Poor security is often claimed as another aspect of the open, transparent file structure, as it is not feasible to 'hide' files or completely prevent unauthorised access. However, it is necessary to know the directory architecture which reduces the risk from unskilled users, and UNIX internal systems do represent a method of preventing unauthorised access. In the US, additional software packages for security are a common system feature. There was no record locking in earlier versions of UNIX, but SVID-based versions and UNIX V.3 and later have this facility. Record and file locking applies across RFS systems.

Security covers both accidental and deliberate damage to the system. To the system owner, the most important item is probably the data held in the system and here UNIX provides good data access which is to an extent the complete absence of protection for data. Anyone can enter the system with the correct password and potentially corrupt the data.

Security is probably best tackled from the physical level so that the most important files cannot be readily corrupted, or can be quickly and safely rebuilt if corruption occurs. It is possible to purchase various additional system utilities to provide security facilities.

Real-time, Parallel Processing and Speed-critical Applications

Although work is continuing on future real-time systems under UNIX, this is not an area where users can easily locate systems capable of tackling these problems. Nor was UNIX ever designed to tackle parallel processing or speed-critical applications. The development of RISC-based machines will certainly increase the potential for higher speeds, and various manufacturers have specialised UNIX flavours and hardware that can run real-time software (often for defence and military purposes) and UNIX-like systems are appearing for parallel processing.

Speed

UNIX is often stated to be too slow for office applications and incapable of supporting sufficient terminals. As remarked above, speed can be improved, and some makes are faster than others with the same load — it is important to choose a hardware mix capable of performing at an appropriate speed and the large numbers of UNIX installations means that it is possible to check other users' experience.

Each terminal user added to a system causes an additional slice of machine to be taken up, and there is also a handling interval so as to ensure that each user gets a fair share. This can slow the response that each user receives at the terminal. The introduction of intelligent workstations that can perform user processes locally (distributed processing) is a technique that can speed up a system, and UNIX can happily support several processors.

FINDING STAFF FOR UNIX SYSTEMS

UNIX has an advantage over most operating systems due to its success in the educational field, as so many computing graduates have been exposed to UNIX. A good proportion, generally the majority, of advertised jobs in the computer press are for contract staff, and for technical skills such as communications and scientific systems. Close examination of employers' requirements reveals that skills most often requested are for applications programmers with good knowledge of database systems such as Informix or Oracle — obviously for system creation or modification.

Although many jobs are advertised for C programmers, these are more likely to be for systems other than UNIX, such as DEC's VMS or DOS. Often it is anticipated that the successful applicant will be able enough and versatile enough to tackle a range of tasks such as support, rather than being a member of a highly specialised programming team. With the expressed preference of the UK government for Posix, there should be increasing opportunity for UNIX skills.

The number of training courses offered on UNIX has increased steadily over the last couple of years, and there has been a considerable increase in graduates with UNIX experience, so there is a reservoir of such skills available.

An important aspect of the success of any system is the right kind of trained staff, and in this area there has been much discussion about shortages of skilled staff. The problem is not helped by the attitudes of many organisations who would rather tempt staff away from other companies than train their own staff. Recruiting can bring the required skills quickly to the company, but a recruitment campaign can cost £2000 for one employee; the same money could buy 16 days of training at £125 (Sharpe, 1986).

Generally, it is a better policy to train existing staff rather than to recruit new staff, because existing staff already know the job and are committed to the company. It can also be expensive to recruit staff, and new staff will take time and effort in training from experienced staff before they become valued company employees. In the computer industry it has been found that the people you train are the people that stay with you, and the trained typist or clerk with aptitude can make a substantial contribution especially for specialist filing jobs such as database management.

It is not always necessary to acquire specialist personnel for operating UNIX workstations, as the majority of high-quality software has been designed to be operated by staff with a minimum of training. Obviously there are tasks that will require specialists, such as program development and communications.

Trained staff with specialist skills are valuable to other companies, and so may be poached away, but the computer industry values experience over training, so the recently trained employee will probably need to gain a couple of years experience before considering moving on or be seen to be attractive to prospective employers. Thus at a minimum it should be possible to get two years of value from the company-trained specialist.

Then there is the choice between recruiting permanent staff or employing personnel on short-term contracts. The computer industry has a large body of specialists who will work as contractors, who tend to be better paid than permanent staff, and are very experienced, competent and with a proven record of successful projects completed. Contract staff skills are naturally for IBM, ICL, and DEC mainframes where the largest proportion of work is to be found, but there are some contractors specialising in UNIX.

Manuals and training materials provided with software have an important role to play, but they often require too much imagination and understanding from staff who have only recently been introduced to office technology. A better policy is to provide a level of training to selected staff members and use them as a cadre for training others. The cadre, together with manuals and training materials, can then provide a help service to the whole company. An environment of competence and self-reliance will draw inexperienced staff into line with their experienced colleagues (Harnett, 1985).

When computers and office automation are introduced, it is often found that a group of staff emerges with both some computer skills and an extensive knowledge of the company's business. These people tend to be the first to discover any technical problems with the system because they will be running the system close to its performance limits. They are also the people most likely to attempt to find and exploit short cuts such as menu by-passes. These people are also the group making most demands on technical specialists, because they are the first to encounter errors or flaws in the system, and so will be looking for answers to a variety of highly technical questions.

The technical specialists are needed to run and develop the main system, so it is worthwhile using a mixture of specialists and trained users, with experience of the system, to provide a help-desk. The experienced users are good recruits for this type of team, because they can relate their own experiences to those of new users, without being blinkered by purely technical considerations. This team can also be invaluable for providing documentation, training and ultimately all internal support for the system.

The skills and experience found in the team make it ideal to estimate the viability of any project expansion, and to determine resources required. As one of the team's roles is responding to user enquiries, it is in an excellent position for monitoring company progress in technology, and finding areas where improvements can be made. There will also be feedback (from user problems to the company policy) that can be employed to modify or enhance the policy. With time, the system will become so well understood that the information centre can supply a first-line diagnostic service and rapidly develop techniques to handle simple but regular problems. Advanced understanding of the hardware and software provides insights that permit the maximum utility to be obtained from the system. For example, software utilities aimed specifically at the whole company can be developed.

It will often be found that flaws or weaknesses are found as users become more expert; the information centre can investigate these problems and develop techniques to resolve the situation. The team may also be valuable to write special company manuals and handbooks to suit company needs or special uses.

6   UNIX in Use

WHO ARE UNIX USERS?   WHAT ARE THE APPLICATIONS?

At the beginning of 1987 it was estimated by Frost and Sullivan that there were 500,000 UNIX systems worldwide. A survey from Datapro and *Computer Weekly* in March 1987 indicated that only 5.2% of mini and 5.8% of mainframe users expected to take on UNIX during 1987. However, in the US, Infocorp estimate that UNIX has 27% of the multi-user market, and predict that this share will rise to 38% within five years; this compares with 40% for proprietary operating systems.

Frost and Sullivan give an installed base in Europe of 40,500 systems in 1986, with a value of nearly $1500 million. In the UK the installed base was about 10,000 systems with a value of $369 million. The author estimates 15,000 systems currently (March 1988), with only about 4,500 in educational or government.

A *Computer News* estimate of the situation by 1991 gave numbers of UNIX systems in the UK as over 140,000, with France having 136,000 and West Germany 150,000. For Europe, the total was over 650,000 units. From these figures, it seems likely that a sizeable proportion of this volume will be micros, using XENIX or the anticipated version of UNIX for the 80386 chip.

A report by Unigram Products in 1987, 'UNIX in the UK', gives a range of interesting statistics. The report was based on telephone interviews with 100 UNIX users in early 1987. This report estimates that there were between 8,000 and 10,000 UNIX installations in the UK, with an average terminal population of 14. The majority of systems were running accounting and word processing packages.

The author's estimates vary from the major surveys as an attempt has been made to include XENIX sites where the majority of applications are used in a full, multi-user system of the same type as a UNIX system, as XENIX is a flavour of UNIX. The majority of UNIX user sites visited by the author were systems installed to handle a specific business problem. Very few users visited had converted from an existing mainframe or mini environment using a different or proprietary operating system, to UNIX. Many systems were intended as more effective versions of micro and PC projects which were not capable of the desired performance.

One of the points of importance is the availability of good software. For example, SMART is a leading MS-DOS product with about 25,000 users in UK. When this package is ported to a UNIX system the users will need no retraining to use the UNIX version which will also offer multi-user and multi-tasking.

A 'STANDARD' USER?

It is very hard to describe a 'standard user', especially considering the range of applications and companies seen; but a 'user profile' can be said to be a comparatively small to medium size company or department, of 20 to 60 staff members, using around six terminals. The majority of software in use across the whole system is a packaged product, but there will be a special software item or file type which is unique to the company. These organisations commonly had no skilled DP personnel attached to the UNIX-based system, and only the larger organisations had arranged user training.

One of the most cogent reasons for adopting UNIX is the ability of a purchaser to change to a totally different make of hardware without an enormous conversion task. An example of this type of conversion site is SDL of Sidcup, who distribute Atari computer products. SDL replaced their PDP 11/44, running Ultrix, by a Convergent Technology S/640 running under UNIX. The PDP was running slowly with about 25 terminals attached, but SDL decided to select the S/640 rather than go up to a VAX processor due to the high cost compared to the performance. SDL's program suites, comprising 75,000 lines of Micro Focus Cobol and running under SCO's XENIX V, were simply recompiled to run on the S/640.

A recently published conversion from one UNIX hardware system to another was reported by Record Data, a US company, who switched from AT&T 3B15 to Sequent Balance 8 hardware in less than two days. The old system was closed down on a Friday and the new machines were working smoothly by Monday, in spite of some minor hardware malfunctions.

UK GOVERNMENT INSTALLATIONS

UK government departments will be buying UNIX systems because the Central Computer and Telecommunications Agency (CCTA), who provide a purchasing protocol for government departments, have instituted a system that requires all suppliers to conform to Posix. CCTA have endorsed UNIX by the adoption of the Posix interface and the X/Open portability guide. The CCTA selected UNIX because it fits in with the Open Systems Initiative (OSI) and more particularly to GOSIP (Government OSI Profile), which is the preferred policy to achieve open systems throughout governmental systems. The applications portability protects investment in software; there will be reduced conversion costs; and the adoption of a standard operating system sidesteps the need to retrain users, development and maintenance staff.

The Commission of the European Communities (CEC) are adopting a procurement policy covering Posix (IEEE 1003.1) and the X/Open collaboration. The Foreign and Commonwealth Office have a system called FOLIOS in place, which is XENIX based.

Central Government's acceptance of the virtues of a unified non-proprietary operating system has been anticipated by several groups of public services including the Metropolitan Police and the armed forces. For example, the Metropolitan Police system called TOPSY (Metropolitan Police Territorial Operations System) provides support facilities for 90 police stations. The Metropolitan Police developed software which was easily ported to different makes of hardware. Applications packages include Q-Office and Informix.

The CCTA internal system MITSY (Main Information Technology System) provides office automation, computing and information needs. The growth paths and easy links of UNIX can give better internal communications within CCTA which facilitates the availability of information databases throughout the organisation. Application packages installed include Q-Office, Informix and Logistix. The system includes an external badge verification system and some additional operating system security. The system is mainly based on Olivetti hardware.

DEFENCE AND SERVICE APPLICATIONS

The Royal Navy are installing the OASIS 4 worldwide logistics system, for stores administration, correspondence management and cash accounts. Gould Computer Systems are supplying hardware with a UNIX-based operating system for this project. Ruggedised minicomputers will be installed in some 50 Royal Navy vessels, with another ten in shore-based support sites. Gould have supplied hardware previously for the OASIS 3 for shore-based installations.

TIS have supplied the Fleet Air Arm school at HMS Daedalus with a UNIX-based training system for teaching ADP skills. Application software supplied includes: comms and terminal emulators; Informix/SQL relational database; Quadratron's office automation package; and desktop publishing from Ventura. Hardware for Daedalus is based on a Convergent Technology S/220 linked to three network PCs running under MS-DOS. The PCs can run as stand-alone machines or be easily linked to the main UNIX box. This yields the advantages of the huge range of MS-DOS software, with relatively easy access to the school-wide system.

A major system is being planned for the Ministry of Defence (MoD) called CHOTS (Corporate Headquarters Office Technology System). The MoD has offended DEC by stating only 100% compliance with UNIX System V will be considered, whereas DEC believe that a bid based on Posix is an equally qualified bid, as Posix is the effective standard aimed at.

RETAILERS

The Retail Management Development Programme (RMDP) survey found that UNIX was used by 24% of all retail packages in 1987, compared with 3% in 1985. In comparison Pick and DOS were used by 3% each, and proprietary operating systems accounted for 28%. MS-DOS achieved 27% and PC-DOS 36%.

The newspaper retailer, John Menzies, has installed over 200 UNIX systems in its branch offices for stock control. The stock control system was written using a fourth-generation language, and the use of UNIX makes it possible for the company to hold only a single version of the program, spread over the range of different types and sizes of machines.

LOCAL AUTHORITIES

Wandsworth Borough Council are one of the first local authorities to select systems based on UNIX. The council chose UNIX to give access to modern, attractive and user friendly software, with reduced dependence on operating system management. Further reasons are: good quality office systems, the wide variety of hardware vendors and support for open systems interconnection, which is an important item for Wandsworth to cover future LAN/WAN links to outlying service departments and depots. UNIX also provides easy links to PCs, and easy spreading of standard applications software over departments. The packaged software in use is Q-Office, Informix, Uniplex 11 and Access 20/20.

East Hampshire District Council is installing ICL DRS 300 processors running under UNIX with IBM-PC compatible ICL PWS workstations. The ICL machines communicate with the existing Honeywell DPS 7 mainframe using Daton proprietary software, and with each other using ICL's OSLAN local area network. The Uniplex integrated office systems software is used on the DRS systems.

APPLICATION BINARY INTERFACES

A method is emerging of running application software across any system designed around a particular architecture without recompiling. The method is termed application binary interface (abi) and Intel, Motorola and Sun are all working hard to deliver an abi for the new UNIX System V version 4.0. The use of an abi is still somewhat controversial as it will mean that applications will be tied to a particular hardware architecture such as a particular chip set, so software will have to be purpose written for the Intel 80386, Sun's Sparc or the Motorola 68030 (Ireland & Neesham, 1988).

The intention is that all abi definitions will comply with AT&T's System V Interface Definition (SVID) and Posix. Unfortunately, none of the abi definitions are backward compatible with previous chip generations, although as chip families tend to build on previous generations there is generally some internal compatibility.

IBM USERS AND UNIX

George Goodwin, of the IBM Computer Users Association, claimed during March 1987 that very few IBM users run UNIX. His view is that IBM is trying to implement a policy that will permit it to compete for tenders where Posix or UNIX are essential; ie in government and educational where very large projects are generated. Another view was expressed by Shaku Atre, of Atre International, who believes that IBM is supporting UNIX as a contingency plan in case the Systems Application Architecture (SAA) is not successful. AIX, IBM's UNIX flavour, does not conform to SAA, which is the so-called 'master plan' for an applications port across the whole IBM hardware range. IBM have committed considerable resources to AIX, and have been running a major advertising campaign in professional magazines over 1987 and 1988.

IBM is a founder member of the Open Software Foundation and AIX is forming the basis for future products. IBM can therefore be seen to be providing future UNIX-based products, but the latest hardware range from IBM, the so-called Silverlake range, does not support UNIX as the main operating system.

CASE STUDIES

These case studies are included to show how UNIX systems are used in various industrial sectors. As one company reported a number of problems involving consultants and hardware suppliers they specifically requested anonymity; this policy has also been applied to the other case studies, although this will in no way detract from the benefits to be gained from such user experience.

Plastic and Resin Moulders

A company producing a wide range of specialised plastic and resin mouldings were seeking to rationalise several office systems that had evolved in isolation. For example, letters to customers were produced on a typewriter after customer details, name and address, had been extracted from a simple order processing system running on an IBM-PC. The order processing system had no provision for easy generation of customer letters. The PC was only single-user, so if several letters to different customers were required, then account addresses would be printed off and then retyped.

Other systems in use were based on PCs for normal accounting and VAT, payroll for the total of 68 employees, and an elaborate shop-floor materials estimating package.

The directors decided to attempt to integrate systems, partly to ensure a single data source was used so that customers' letters did not go the wrong customer (which had happened!), but more importantly, so that it would be possible for managers to assess future slack periods well in advance. A senior manager was given the job of assessing requirements for a suitable computing system that would tackle all of the existing jobs and also provide the job scheduling function. It was at first considered possible to link all the PCs together with a file server, and upgrade the size and capacities to improve performance. The manager visited a few computer shows and read a great deal of technical material, but was at first unable to get to grips with the task until a salesman suggested a suitable software package for job scheduling running on a small minicomputer.

After reporting to the directors, the manager's estimates of cost were assessed and it became obvious that although the initial cost was high in relationship to the costs of the individual PCs, the overall costs were lower than the cost of upgrading the PCs to tackle the tasks. A further point was that the size of the mini was reckoned to be adequate to handle the other administrative functions.

The directors asked a consultant to confirm their findings, before committing themselves to the expenditure. The consultant was in general agreement, but suggested that, by selecting a slightly larger machine, it would be possible to run all requirements concurrently under UNIX. It was found then that the preferred job scheduling system was available in a UNIX version that included easy links to other office functions, so the decision was taken to purchase the consultant's recommendations.

Installation was rapid, but considerable time was wasted because the consultant had stated that the PCs could be used as terminals, which turned out to be only partly true as the PCs did not function correctly until additional boards were fitted internally. This pushed up costs and, because the system had given considerable problems to staff, reduced the employees' willingness to accept the system.

When the complete system was finally running without snags, the directors asked for a full review of the installation. During the presentation of the review, the systems manager pointed out that no provision had been made for day-to-day operations management, but the system was running well, and the number of complaints from users had continued to decline. The majority of users also thought that the system was a vast improvement on the PCs. An attempt was made to generate a cost/benefits comparison, but it was found difficult to prove a cost reduction. However, the integration of the originally separate systems was well liked by the management team, and the enhanced job scheduling could be shown to improve factory floor machine usage. The directors believe that, in the long term, the system will increase competitiveness, especially as several British and foreign competitors have expressed considerable interest in the computer system!

Leathergoods Retailer

This organisation controls the running of six shops in the Kent and Sussex area, selling mainly shoes and leathergoods but also some handicrafts items. Orders are placed with manufacturers and wholesalers considerably in advance; for example, some types of shoe can take six months between order and delivery. Two major suppliers are based in Italy, and paperwork requirements for international trade are an enormous strain on the company.

About 100 employees work at a total of nine sites (including shop premises), and sites are spread over a large area; it is 90 miles between the farthest spread points. The decision was made in 1984 to link together the sites so as to allow any shop to call upon the stock from all other sites. Although technically this was feasible, and telephone links were established, the system was used for simple enquiries from one shop assistant speaking directly to another. This resulted in even more paperwork to cover inter-shop stock transfers.

In 1986 a minicomputer was installed, running under UNIX, at the head office. This machine was intended to provide a stock control and order processing system to cover the buying of stock from the UK and Ireland, but was under-utilised because procedures became simplified. The DP manager, who had been with the company for many years working in a different role, looked around for something more for the mini to do, and decided to try to exploit the site telephone links. A contractor was employed to devise a stock report system, which was not initially linked to the stock control system. Three secondhand terminals were installed at the larger shops, and a trial period of three months showed significant improvements in the stock transfer system.

After the trial, a multi-user stock control package was purchased which proved reasonably successful, but was disliked by the staff who preferred the original system created by the contractor. Eventually a front-end resembling the original system was grafted on to improve staff acceptance.

At the time of writing, the mini is regarded as obsolete and worn-out, and an off-the-shelf solution to handle all office procedures is being investigated. However, the consensus opinion of staff and management is that the old system worked well and was easily learned, but was very unfriendly if anything went wrong. In the early days there had also been some disasters with file corruption, due to inadequate file protection and back-up. The purchased multi-user stock control system was working so well that most users were unaware that the system had been significantly changed.

Cost justification is possible with this system as it was proved that at least ten extra staff members would have been needed to operate the improved stock transfer system. As hardware and software totalled £170,000, and the jobs would have cost about £68,000 per year, the computer system became cost effective by the third year. This is a simplistic view, because it does negate the running costs of the system and the value of the staff displaced from other tasks to assist with installation and operation of the system. However, as the DP manager says, the system has proved its worth in terms of productivity and competitiveness.

Software House

It is noticeable that a large proportion of UNIX sites develop software, either for internal use or as the main product of the company. This case study is from a company that specialises in the development of accounting packages for general business use. The language originally used was Cobol, but now more software is being created using C.

The company started up in 1983, at first using a minicomputer running under the maker's proprietary operating system. This restricted sales to users with similar machines, especially as non-compatible versions of the same operating system were used on larger and smaller models of the same make. The situation came to a head after the manufacturer introduced upgrades to the operating system that further restricted compatibility.

The software house had by this time installed about twenty software systems, and wanted to expand the business to cover a wider range of machines. The answer seemed to lie in selecting a non-proprietary operating system, or an operating system in extremely widespread use. Effectively the choice came down to UNIX, Pick, BOS or MS-DOS. MS-DOS was rejected as it would be difficult for the company to quickly enter the mass production and distribution arena essential for success in this highly competitive field, and profit margins would be slim, restricting future development unless high volume sales could be quickly achieved.

This left the multi-user systems, UNIX, Pick and BOS. As UNIX was much in the news at this point, a hardware system was selected that supported UNIX System V, although many of the staff believed that the Berkeley System would have been more suitable, because of the better networking facilities. At that time, it was considered that Pick and BOS were available on too few makes of hardware. Therefore, after taking advice from a number of sources, System V was chosen, and it was found possible to take some 'advanced orders' from customers wishing to expand their existing systems.

The chosen system supported ten terminals initially, with a large disk capacity. Development continued using Cobol, and each development group was provided with an individual set of directories. Within each group's directories were test data, the individual programs under development, and a single data dictionary, all of which were available to the programmers within that group. Programs were also divided into blocks of work so that several programmers could simultaneously work on the same project. This aspect is still regarded by the company as the best feature of UNIX systems.

There are now eighteen terminals attached to the system, fourteen of which are used for software development. The remaining four are used for software support and long-term research for future products. The system is well-liked by its users, whose biggest gripe is the comparatively slow speed of compilation, even with quite small program modules. This is not a significant problem, as it was allowed for in the original specification, but it does annoy programmers.

No attempt has been made to cost-justify the system, as the management are aware that the company would probably have ceased to trade if they had continued with the previous system.

7   UNIX Hardware Suppliers

THE SPECTRUM OF SUPPLIERS

This chapter looks at the various implementations of UNIX from suppliers. Because there are so many suppliers, and because there is a continual increase in the numbers of suppliers providing a UNIX version or a UNIX flavour, it is rather easier to say who is not supplying but in a fast-changing world that would quickly become incorrect. Therefore, this chapter will deal with specific examples of UNIX and UNIX-like operating systems that are available in the UK. This cannot be taken as a comprehensive list, as only a few examples are included and new suppliers are appearing weekly; also any comment on the features and facilities in a particular version are contemporary with the writing of this book in late 1988.

First, it must be said that C does not guarantee UNIX; a hardware configuration which can support the C language does not necessarily provide or support UNIX. UNIX system utilities are written in C but the kernel is machine-specific. There are a range of (mainly) scientific micro and minicomputers which provide C as a matter of course but will not run UNIX due to insufficient disk and memory space or because the processor cannot provide the system kernel.

Again, although UNIX is described as a multi-user operating system it does not have to be used in this way and there are several applications systems set up as essentially single-user but offering a measure of multi-tasking facilities.

Most UNIX-type systems seem to attempt to retain a flavour of UNIX in the name, even if it's only an 'x'; for example, DUX from Hewlett-Packard, Ultrix from DEC, AIX from IBM, OSx from Pyramid, and A/UX from Apple. The origin of versions and the resemblance of a particular supplier's version to the original is very hard to define (and changes often), especially when 'user-friendly' front-ends have been grafted on, but most implementations are based on versions later than UNIX System III, and the commonest start point is UNIX System V, usually the SVID.

The most popular UNIX look-alike in terms of numbers sold is Microsoft's XENIX, which was developed from UNIX System III, incorporating an improved front-end, full and careful debugging and an excellent re-documentation exercise. The XENIX operating system is available on a number of large micros, including the IBM PC-AT.

The characteristic ease of porting to new machines has provoked a downward spread of UNIX to the PC world, where the much more powerful processors such as the Intel 80386 (also known as the 386) and Motorola 68030 need better operating systems to run much larger sizes of store. Although Concurrent DOS from Digital Research was successful in the 1 to 4 user micro market, it cannot handle the memory address range of UNIX. Several other proprietary operating systems are also competing in this field, but they do not have the backing of the hundreds of software and hardware suppliers with UNIX products.

Novon Research Group estimated that the leading UNIX flavours worldwide in 1987 were as shown in Table 7.1.

Berkeley 4.x	2043
UNIX System V	1500
XENIX	623
Uniplus	186
Others	1083
Total	5435

Table 7.1   Value of UNIX Flavours Worldwide 1987 (in $millions)

Some idea of price/performance can be illustrated by the Mips M1000 machine which cost £100,000 (November 1987) for a 32 terminal system. The M1000 can support up to 100 users running at 10 million instructions per second, with 16Mb of internal memory and 300Mb of disk storage.

Unisys, formed by the merging of Burroughs and Sperry, are major suppliers of UNIX-based machines, from workstations to full-power mainframes. Unisys UNIX is compatible with UNIX V.2 throughout the range.

Apricot have made XENIX available on their XEN-i range since the launch of these machines, based on UNIX V.2. A number of office automation packages are available for these systems, which can handle up to 16 users. Selecting XENIX has permitted Apricot to offer systems supporting from one to a thousand users, with easy expansion paths and software that remains compatible across the whole range.

ICL have a strong commitment to UNIX to fit into their strategy of VME for corporate computing, UNIX for departmental computing and DOS for personal computing. This provides overlap and cross-linking using simple tools. VME can host UNIX within the same system, and ICL's range includes the Clan, System 25 and DRS machines, all of which can run with UNIX as the host. ICL use a version of UNIX conforming to UNIX System V.2 and to X/Open standards.

Olivetti, with close links to AT&T, use 'real' UNIX V.3 on the 3B2/400 range.

HP-DUX is the flavour of UNIX from Hewlett-Packard, and is based on SVID-2. However, Hewlett-Packard have also made its entire range of office services software available under its own proprietary operating system as well as under UNIX. There will also be a Windows interface through which MS-DOS and OS/2 systems will be able to run UNIX applications.

Siemens supply Sinix on the MX500 range that runs from a single user to 96 user workstations, and guarantees running of software on upgraded systems without changes. Sinix is based on UNIX System V and XENIX V3.0. This range is based on National Semiconductor's NS 32032 32-bit microprocessors.

Atari launched a machine in 1988 which is based on the VME-bus, using the Motorola 68030 chip running at 20MHZ. This machine uses the UNIX V version 3.1 operating system, with NFS file sharing, and can support up to 20 terminals.

Abaq have created a parallel processor system using 13 Inmos Transputer T800 processor chips, which uses the UNIX-like Helios operating system written by Perihelion. This was claimed to be the only operating system in use so far for Transputers; the operating system is written in C and supports Occam, a specialist programming language for parallel processing. A new operating system for Transputers is called Hobbes, supplied by Transoft, and it also uses C but is not UNIX compatible, nor does it support Occam.

Prime's model EWS PXCL5500 runs UNIX System V.3 (extended), and Prime have a UNIX flavour called Primix running under the proprietary PRIMOS operating system. However, Prime are developing a native version of UNIX for the 50 series, the flagship of the range. A native version has been available on the EXL supermicro series for some while, but Prime have decided to offer UNIX so as to provide a common environment across the whole model range, and hopefully pick up some tenders from central government who are demanding Posix conformance.

IBM started in the UNIX field with an operating system for the 370 range called IX/370 (IX for Interactive Executive), and another operating system called S/1 IX running on the Series 1 minis. The PC AT offered UNIX in two different versions, one being another version of IX and the other operating system was Microsoft's XENIX. However, most users stayed with DOS.

Another UNIX flavour, ACIS, is available on the versions of the RT PC sold to universities. IBM also have a 'secure' version of UNIX called C2.0, intended for defence applications (Babcock, 1987).

IBM's current flavour of UNIX is called AIX, for Advanced Interactive Executive. AIX and 386/IX for the Intel 80386 chip are products from Interactive Systems, now owned by Kodak. The 6150 PC RT micro runs AIX with about 400 applications and IBM are moving AIX to compliance with Posix. Further, IBM are developing a migration path from IX370, the version of UNIX available on the 30XX and 43XX machines, to AIX. IBM plans to implement AIX across the range from the PS2 model 80 to the 9370, 4381 and 3090 mainframes using vector processors. AIX will also run on the 370 mainframe range. There are no plans to integrate AIX with SAA, or support AIX under SAA, but there will be an overlap, possibly as high as 90% of the hardware range. Migration by users from IX/370 to AIX will start during 1988 as products for the PS/2 range become available.

Wang's UNIX-based product called IN/ix was written in collaboration with Interactive Systems, who also collaborated with IBM on the AIX system. IN/ix is compliant with SVID and will comply with Posix when that has been completely established. TCP/IP networking will also be included. IN/ix will run in Wang's VS/Virtual Machine.

Pyramid's hardware ranges for the 9805, 9810, 9820, 9830 and 9840 models use a RISC based architecture running the OSx operating system to support Berkeley 4.2 BSD and UNIX System V.

DEC's Ultrix has features of both SVID and Berkeley 4.2 but is not necessarily compatible with either. However, DEC also have a version of VMS, the proprietary operating system, which will comply with Posix. DEC claimed that 10,000 Ultrix systems have been sold worldwide.

Ultrix is based on the Berkeley 4.2, which conflicts with Apple who have AT&T's System V version 2.2 as the underlying basis of A/UX. This may cause problems, as the two companies have a close working relationship after the merger in 1987. A/UX also contains elements from the Berkeley (BSD) versions 4.2 and 4.3, and Sun NFS (Network File System) with TCP/IP. The Apple Macintosh will also be able to run A/UX.

Zilog, the manufacturers of the Z80 chip, have moved to the AT&T 32-bit chip and are committed to UNIX systems, basing the System 8000/32 on UNIX System V with over 500 applications packages. The Motorola 68000 family can also run UNIX.

Amdahl is a manufacturer of IBM compatible mainframes and supply the UTS operating system, a version of UNIX System V, which is used at one of Britain's largest UNIX sites (ATP — AT&T/Philips Telecommunications) for 150 software developers to create and develop software for the 5ESS telephone exchange for Freephone numbers. Current Amdahl version is UTS/V, which is an SVID compatible version of the original UTS/580.

Cray use a version of UNIX called UniCOS which is currently the operating system supplied for the giant Cray 2. Cray's own proprietary operating system, COS, is no longer being developed.

Altos have a merged UNIX/XENIX operating system called UNIX V/386 for the Intel 80386-based Series 1000. V/386 is fully compatible with UNIX V Release 6 and also includes features of XENIX. Altos plan the Series 2000 machines using the 386 chip that can support up to 100 users. Altos do not sell directly to customers, but only through a network of value-added resellers; this ensures a greater competence from the dealer which is needed for the more complex networking and multi-user applications.

UNIX AND THE DEALER

Multi-user software requires a greater commitment from the dealer, both in terms of capital and in terms of support over a longer term than for most PC products. UNIX does require software skills from the software house, although UNIX porting is claimed to be relatively simple. UNIX will also cost more than many proprietary operating systems in the first instance, but subsequent addition of extra users may cost as little as £600.

The unfriendliness of UNIX to the user is not noticed by most users who can easily exploit database packages such as Informix and office automation packages such as Q-Office, which do not require any knowledge of the operating system. One of the reasons why UNIX is becoming more acceptable is the huge range of high quality, easy-to-use packages coming on to the market.

8   UNIX Versus Other Non-Proprietary Operating Systems

INTRODUCTION

This chapter looks at the opposition to UNIX in order to focus attention on the areas where UNIX has not done well, as well as on those features that make UNIX successful. As with other aspects of UNIX, it is hard to define technical features and compare them with other operating systems, as there are so many versions and flavours of UNIX.

The operating systems discussed in this chapter are merely the most popular in terms of availability and sales, without reference to type or size of systems capable of using the operating system.

UNIX VERSUS PICK

The effort going into a standard for UNIX shows the commitment of suppliers to UNIX. Few other operating systems have received the same level of sustained interest as UNIX, but for a considerable period Pick, the brainchild of Richard Pick, has been a competitor. Pick is available on Honeywell, and McDonnell Douglas hardware, amongst others, and there are many Pick installations in the UK health service and local government. Pick offers the hardware independence of Unix with currently over 20 manufacturers offering it. There is also the same aspect of protection of software investment offered by UNIX.

Pick has highly efficient system usage which is optimised to suit hardware, virtual storage management, and an efficient database manager. Variable length data records keep storage volumes tight and it can run big applications on smaller kit due to the effectiveness of memory management.

A further feature is upward compatibility as versions for smaller machines can be portable to larger machines and other makes without conversion. A dictionary system allows the terms familiar to users to be used as data names. Flexibility of data storage comes from the variable record sizing and storing of adjacent data in adjacent areas.

The system gives a comprehensive report generating system for prints using built-in tools and an enquiry system for ad-hoc reports (Bourdon 1986).

So why hasn't Pick succeeded? To begin with, Pick is not so heavily advertised as UNIX, as there are fewer manufacturers offering the product. McDonnell Douglas, one of the leading Pick suppliers, also tend to emphasise applications solutions rather than the operating system. A supplier buys UNIX and adds bits to suit; Pick is installed on a machine 'as is', as few extensions can be added. Pick is not much used by universities so there is no creation of a new generation of dedicated Pick users in the same way as UNIX.

Against this, Pick can run on 68000-based micros. A French company, Intertechnique Informatique (IN2 Ltd in UK) have a C compiler. There is only one, standard, version of Pick, supplied by the Pick organisation, and compatibility is therefore assured. Pick includes an integrated database management system and programmer development tools. Pick and UNIX can complement each other, and it is possible for both to co-exist on the same machine. A product called UniVerse provides a system running under UNIX that is compatible and can run Pick programs. This is currently available on NCR machines.

Pick and UNIX combined would yield over 3000 applications to the user from Pick and at least the same number for UNIX. There would also be available many high performance communications and software development tools from UNIX (Errington, 1988).

UNIX VERSUS BOS

BOS (Business Operating System) is a British product that has been gaining acceptance from users and suppliers over the past five years. It is available over a wide range of hardware sizes from micros to minis, but has not achieved the sales of either UNIX or Pick. There are many reasons for this, but the combination of the limited number of software products and the limited number of hardware manufacturers endorsing BOS is probably the most significant point.

UNIX AND PC-DOS

MS/PC-DOS is the most widely used operating system for PCs, with millions of installations and thousands of applications packages. Although PC-DOS may soon be superseded by the new OS/2 operating system, these millions of PCs will still exist. It is feasible to connect PCs to UNIX so as to permit interworking of DOS and UNIX, with a transparent interface so that users can access files from the UNIX environment. This enables the evolution of complete networks of PCs and UNIX to give both local processing power and remote file access.

Applications are already available in the US to interwork OS/2 and UNIX.

9   The Future of UNIX

GENERAL

This chapter gives some information on the likely future developments in the UNIX world, especially in terms of the standards situation. The various implementations of UNIX-like systems such as AIX are likely to become absorbed into the OSF product, which as yet has no distinctive name; then there is the Posix system and finally the AT&T products may well form another separate group of products. There are therefore three strands of the potential future growth.

UNIX has been increasing its user base by 50% per year over the last three years, and seems all set to continue doing so over the next five years. At the beginning of 1987 it was estimated by Frost and Sullivan that there were 500,000 UNIX systems worldwide. The report predicted that the UNIX market would grow to 16 times its size in 1987 by 1991; with the value of European installations increasing from $1.5 billion at the end of 1986 to $24 billion in 1991. The number of UNIX systems will increase from 40,500 to 67,000. Frost and Sullivan's report emphasised the vital role of standards in making UNIX more attractive to users, and also the feeling in the user community that open systems were becoming more important. The report also mentions the great value of the roles of organisations such as X/ Open in resolving standards problems.

Infocorp report that in 1982 UNIX held only 9.5% of the multi-user market. By 1987 this had risen to more than 27% and Infocorp estimate this will rise to 38.6%.

Encore, a US company specialising in parallel processing systems, has ported an operating system called Mach on to their Multimax machines, which is claimed represents the future of UNIX. Mach has been developed by Carnegie-Mellon University using Department of Defense funding as the operating system for a 'superfast' parallel system capable of executing one billion instructions per second (1000 mips).

Mach is not an extension or a special version of UNIX, but started out as Berkeley UNIX on DEC VAX machines. Mach runs on Encore's Multimax range of signal processing and image processing systems. Mach retains UNIX compatibility and is said to be easy to port over a range of modern microprocessors.

Wang and Plexus have UNIX-based document image processing systems, moving UNIX on to the future office processing ideas that will permit plain paper input of old data files and the creation of electronic systems for retrieval of the archived records. As with the PC, there are a number of other 'future technology' ideas being first implemented on UNIX systems.

If international standards can be established for UNIX, and these standards are accepted by the user base, then UNIX stands an excellent chance of becoming the dominant multi-user operating system. The standards effort is happening, so it is highly likely that UNIX will become predominant, even to the extent of overtaking proprietary systems.

Sun's SPARC chip set is seen as a significant event in UNIX terms because it suggests that the link between Sun and AT&T may tend to produce new SPARC-based versions of UNIX; previous versions were tied originally to DEC hardware sets, and later on Western Digital (an AT&T company) 32000 series chips, which in both cases did not particularly worry other hardware suppliers. However, if UNIX now is to be sold for a special chip set obtainable only through a major UNIX manufacturer, other companies feel that UNIX hardware independence is compromised.

Sun Microsystems announced a product called 'Open Look' in April 1988 which provides a windowing interface to UNIX, intended to make UNIX as easy to use as the Apple Macintosh.

There is likely to be considerable spin-over into the micro arena for UNIX on the 80386-based machines which seem poised to become the new *de facto* standard, as OS/2 has not received a rapturous reception. Although most users' real requirements on these micros seem to be for multi-tasking, or what Rank Xerox called 'windows', so that one user can move quickly from one task to another without closing down the first task, the latest generation of operating systems are probably harder to master than UNIX. If UNIX appears with an easy interface and plenty of links for networking and file transfers, it would be very attractive for a large number of micro users.

AT&T's System V release 4.0 will also conform to Posix and covers the System V interface definition and X/Open's Common Application Environment.

CONCLUSIONS

Like Henry Ford's Model T, UNIX may not be the top performer or even the product most suitable for many applications, but it shares at least two major virtues with the Tin Lizzy: it is highly adaptable and readily available.

At the time of writing, the two contentious issues in the UNIX world are the Open Software Foundation and the SPARC systems, neither of which are yet available as visible products. However, while these products will undoubtedly form some part of the future face of UNIX, for the time being UNIX continues to gain sales and tighten its grip on the market.

Appendix 1
Glossary

4GL, 4th GLs	4th-generation Languages are programming systems that assist users in creating applications software.
AIX	Advanced Interactive Executive, an operating system available on IBM 370 series, RT6150 and PS/2 series.
Algorithm	A solution to a problem, based on a set of precisely defined rules.
ANSI	American National Standards Institute.
Application	A specific purpose or task.
Archiving	Saving data for an indefinite but long period.
ASCII	American Standard Code on Information Interchange. Generally pronounced 'askey'. A coding system that uses 7 *bits* to hold all alphabetic, numerical and punctuation symbols used in English, together with some special message control symbols such as start and end of transmission, carriage return and linefeed. 7 bits hold 127 different values, so a single *byte* has room for an additional 128 symbols.
B	Computer language which developed into C.
Back-up	A copy of a disk, file or record that can be used instead of the original if disaster strikes. Back-up can be applied to a whole range of techniques available to resolve all types of failure.
BASIC	*B*eginners *A*ll-purpose *S*ymbolic *I*nstruction *C*ode. A simple programming language.
Berkeley	The University of California at Berkeley, CA.
Binary	Number system with base of 2. Value of a *bit* can only be 0 or 1, but very convenient in computers as value of a bit can be expressed as the presence or absence of a voltage at a specific point; holding a larger range of values, for example by using 0 to 9 volts requires very accurate detection which could cause enormous complications in design and manufacture of computers.
BISON	Association of five European hardware manufacturers (Bull, ICL, Siemens, Olivetti and Nixdorf) which led to X/Open.

Bit — *Binary Dig*it. An invented name for the smallest unit in the binary mathematical system, and also for a magnetic or electrical signal used to represent a bit. Can only be 1 or 0.

Boot, Booting, Bootstrap — Moving the start-up data for an operating system from disk into memory. Boot data is the start-up information telling the computer how to load in the rest of the system. From 'pulling oneself up by one's bootstraps'.

B-Net — Networking system developed by Berkeley.

BSD — Berkeley Software Distribution, a UNIX version developed at Berkeley.

Buffer — A temporary holding area for data.

Bug — An error in *software*.

Bus — An external *bus* is a wire or group of wires that transmit both data and control signals between computer and *peripherals* — some examples are IEEE-488, S-100 and STD. An internal bus is the arrangement of data, control and power lines within a computer, either as a series of circuit board 'tracks' or as connecting wires.

Byte — An IBM-invented name for 8 *bits*. Can hold one of 256 different values (0 to 255) so can hold any English alphabetic symbol. Although numbers can be held in this format, numbers can be handled more efficiently by using special codes such as *EBCDIC*. A byte will often hold an *ASCII* value.

C — A programming language often used in UNIX systems.

CAE — Common Applications Environment. X/Open definition for portable software.

Carriage Return — As with a typewriter, the movement of the paper or screen data up one line, together with movement of the *cursor* to the start of the next line.

Catalog — List of the contents of a disk, and also sometimes the command that displays that catalog. An alternative name is *directory*.

CCITT — Comité Consultatif International Télgraphique et Téléphonique. A UN standards body for communications.

CCTA — Central Computer and Telecommunications Agency. A UK civil service body.

Centronics — A proprietary *parallel* interface designed for Centronics printers, and popular on many makes of personal computers. Based on a 36-way standard connector.

Character Set — Complete collection of all letters, numbers and punctuation marks available for use by a computer input or output device.

Chip — See *Processor chip*.

Chip Family — A group of chips designed to work together, with, say, a *processor chip,* a keyboard control chip, screen handler and disk controller.

C-ISAM — Informix Corporation's version of ISAM (Indexed Sequential Access Method) — a technique for accessing data.

Command — An instruction given to a computer by an operator or by the operating system that has a definite function. May cause the execution of several programs or simply one machine-code instruction.

Compilation Conversion of program from *source code* to a version that can be run on a machine. Output from compilation is called 'object code'.

Compiler Software, usually part of an operating system, that converts a program from source code prepared by programmer into a list of links to internal routines that can be *executed*.

CMOS Complimentary Metal Oxide Silicon. A type of transistor or silicon chip; when used as memory components CMOS uses less power and is capable of retaining contents for long periods if an on-board battery is fitted.

CP/M Control Program for Microcomputers. An operating system for 8-bit micros.

Data Transfer Rate The rate at which data can be transferred from a disk, tape, communications line or computer memory.

Database A group of related files organised for efficient access.

Dedicated A hardware and software package intended for only one function. For example, a dedicated word processor would have keys on the keyboard with specific word processing functions, such as 'new page' or 'end paragraph'.

De facto In standards terms, an acceptance that a particular product is the industry standard.

Directory A library of disk contents. Also, with some operating systems, the command that displays the library (MS-DOS command is DIR, for cxamplc).

DRAM Dynamic *RAM*. Random Access Memory that is continually 'refreshed' by rewriting the contents. Because storage is based on a capacitor, each memory cell can be simplified. See also *SRAM*.

EBCDIC Expanded Binary Coded Decimal Interchange Code. A method for coding decimal numbers to give very high and very low values using very little storage. For instance, values representing 12 to the power of plus or minus 72 can be held in 8 *bytes*.

Edit To amend a record or file, using a special program. Some machines provide editors as part of the operating system, UNIX offers several editors within the system utilities.

EPROM Erasable Programmable Read-only Memory. Storage chips that are written electronically and erased by using an ultra-violet light through a special window in the case. Generally used during development of a new system. See *PROM* and *ROM*.

EEPROM Electronically Erasable Read-only Memory. As *EPROM* but can be erased electronically.

Ergonomics The science of linking human effort to machines.

ESPRIT European Strategic Programme for Research into Information Technology.

Execute To perform a task or obey an instruction.

FCI   Field Changes per Inch. A measure of recording density on magnetic disk or tape.

Field   Part of a record with its own identity, for example, 'address' is a field within each *record* in a telephone directory.

File   Collection of data with common features; group of *records* with same range of contents.

File Controller   The electronic component of a disk drive that executes all disk functions.

File Manager   Part of an operating system that issues all instructions for handling files.

Gigabyte   One thousand, million *bytes* as a convenient expression — actually 1,073,741,823 bytes.

Hardware   Any part of a computer system that can be seen and touched.

Hex   Short for 'hexadecimal'. Numbers to the base of 16; values range from 0 to F. F=15 and occupies 4 *bits*.

Icons   Small pictures used on a screen to represent an activity, for example a picture of a floppy disk might represent all filing activities.

IEE   The Institute of Electrical Engineers (UK).

IEEE   The Institute of Electrical and Electronic Engineers (USA). This body produces standards for electronic devices such as connections between machines. Standards usually carry the Institute's initials — ie IEEE-488. IEEE is often pronounced 'Eye-triple-E' in the UK.

IEEE-488   A standard *parallel* connection method for laboratory equipment or microcomputer peripherals.

Inverted file   An index file containing only a list of data record numbers and a code for the contents of one field from the records.

Intermediate file A file holding data that is required only temporarily. Often used in word processing systems to hold the amendments being made during the editing session, which will form the latest version of the document.

ISAM   Indexed Sequential Access Method. A versatile data storage method using a separate index file carrying addresses of records in the data file.

ISO   International Standards Organisation — also a version of *ASCII* used internationally.

Keyfield   A field in a record uniquely identifying that record; for example customer name, record number, product code. Often used to sort a file into an order, for example sorting names alphabetically.

Kilobyte   Also used are Kb and Kbyte. Actually means 1024 *bytes* but normally spoken of as if meaning one thousand bytes. Computer jargon is 'K', pronounced 'kay'.

Language   Programming language. A special series of words that cause specific events within the computer to occur when the program is run.

Line feed   Movement of paper to the next line, or a *cursor* to the next screen line.

Load a program	To move a program into the main memory so that it can be *executed*.
Megabyte	Also used are Mb and Mbyte. Actually 1024 *Kilobytes* but normally spoken of as if meaning one million bytes. Computer jargon is 'M', pronounced 'meg'.
Mouse	Hand-held device for moving *cursor* or pointer around screen, by pushing over table surface.
MHz	MegaHertz — one million cycles per second.
Microprocessor	See *Processor chip*.
Microsecond	One millionth of a second.
Millisecond	One thousandth of a second.
MS-DOS	Operating system for 16-bit micros.
NBS	American National Bureau of Standards.
NFS	Network File System.
Noise	Undesirable, irregular electrical or acoustic fluctuations accompanying but not relevant to a particular signal.
Parallel data	Data arranged into blocks that permit simultaneous transfer of one block, say one byte. This will require 8 data lines or wires, but gives fast movement of data. See also *Serial*.
Peripheral	A device external to the processor of a computer, such as a printer or disk drive.
Processor chip	The electronic heart of any micro. In mainframe terms, the CPU. A tiny piece of silicon crystal with deliberately introduced lines of impurities that make thousands of transistors on the surface of the crystal. The transistors perform the function of a computer. Processor chips — also called microprocessors — appear in all kinds of electronic equipment, but the most familiar examples are built into microcomputers. Examples of processors are the MOS Technology Inc 6502 used in the Apple, Commodore and BBC, the Intel 8088 used in the IBM-PC, and the Motorola 68000 found in the Sinclair QL, the Atari 520 and the Apple Macintosh.
PSTN	*Public Switched Telephone Network* — the conventional national telephone system.
RAM	Random Access Memory. Internal memory, based on silicon chips, that holds programs, data etc, when the micro is running. The contents are lost if the power is switched off.
Random access file	A file permitting access to any record without reading all previous records.
Record	A part of a file with its own unique identity; for example an individual name, address and telephone number in a telephone directory.
Relative file	A file where all records can be found by a relative displacement from the start point.
RISC	Reduced Instruction Set Computer — a computer architecture that uses very few internal instructions. Although this lowers the versatility of the internal instructions, processing can be much faster.

ROM — Read-only Memory. Internal memory, based on silicon chips, that holds its data permanently. No part of the data can be changed.

RS232 — A very common data transfer standard. This standard describes the signals sent over a cable between 2 computers, and lays down voltages, etc. Normally based on 25-pin, D-type connectors at each end, but can use ordinary telephone wires and be connected to the public telephone network. This is a *Serial* data transfer method.

Serial data — The movement of data one *bit* at a time. Slow but simple and cheap.

Serial file — File where data is entered as it is found; the data will be in the order of entry.

Sequential file — File with records placed in some fixed order using the *keyfield*.

Source code — Program as written in original computer language (ie before compilation).

Spreadsheet — A program such as VISICALC or LOTUS 1-2-3 which displays data as a matrix of entries in columns and rows, like a high electronic sheet of paper. An entry can be a value or a formula using the row and column addresses of values; the result of changing a value can be immediately displayed on the screen.

Sort — Re-order records in a file. Several interesting *Algorithms* exist to produce the shortest route to any desired order; all require the file to be read, shuffled and rewritten.

SRAM — Static *RAM*. Random Access Memory that does not require continual 'refreshment' by rewriting contents every cycle; more complex and expensive than *DRAM* but can be faster and requiring less power.

Storage — 'Memory', a place where data or programs can be stored (and retrieved from). Internal storage is generally based on transistors or silicon chips, external storage is magnetic or optical in nature.

Structured — A technique of program design that yields an easily tested and documented program.

SVID — System V Interface Definition. A description of various features of links to AT&T's UNIX System V.

Synchronisation — With floppy disks, to match speed of disk rotation with specified reading and writing speed. With communications equipment such as modems, synchronisation ensures that both ends of the communications line start 'counting in' or 'counting out' blocks of data simultaneously.

Text file — A file containing text to be displayed on a screen or printed. Usually the simplest type of serial file, but will include control characters for presentation format.

Transparent — Not seen by or concealed from the user.

UNIX — A sophisticated operating system available for many different types of micro and mini computers.

WIMP — *W*indows, *I*cons, *M*ice and *P*ointing systems — systems which use these techniques to make the user interface easier to use.

Windowing — A technique of providing multi-tasking, so that one user can move from one task to another without having to close down each task before moving.

Appendix 2
Bibliography

CHAPTER 1

Cost effective UNIX, *Computers in Defence,* March/April 1988.

Gooding, C, Riding high on the UNIX wave, *Computer Weekly,* 16th July 1987.

CHAPTER 2

Annual Census of UK-Installed Computer Systems, Pedder Associates Ltd, 1987.

Foremski, T, UNIX rises under Posix's wing, *Computing,* 19th February 1987.

CHAPTER 3

Thomas, R, and Yates, J, *A User Guide to the UNIX System,* McGraw-Hill, 1982.

Jones, P, UNIX comes out of its shell, *Informatics,* July 1987.

The UNIX report, Digitus, 1985.

Malone, S, Whose hand on the reins?, *Practical Computing,* July 1987.

CHAPTER 4

Burgess, M K, UNIX, NCC Publications, 1987.

McKee, R, UNIX needs to raise performance, *Computer News,* 22nd October 1987.

Earnest-Jones, T, UNIX agreement opens users' doors, *Computer Weekly,* 28th May 1987.

Earnest-Jones, T, Whitehall looks to portability of UNIX, *Computer Weekly,* 15th October 1987.

Smith, J M, International Standards for the Interchange of Text, *Oxford Surveys in Information Technology,* Oxford University Press, 1985.

Sweet, P, Standards steam ahead, *Computing,* 8th January 1987.

Guest, D, UNIX's standards issue, *Microscope,* 6th April 1988.

Lester, C, Letting Standards Drop, *Informatics,* January 1988.

Manchester, P, UNIX — from here to eternity, *Computing,* 23rd July 1987.

Raymond, M, Heading for harmony in the UNIX universe, *DEC Computing,* 1st April 1987.

CHAPTER 5

Sharpe, R, Learning the value of training, *Network,* November 1986.

Harnett, J, *User's Guide to Office Automation,* 1985.

Hammond, C, A matter of course?, *Practical Computing,* August 1986.

Kolodziej, S, Now C finds a role on the mainframe stage, *Computer News,* 7th April 1988.

Anwyll, J, UNIX transactions, *Systems International,* September 1987.

CHAPTER 6

UNIX Computer Systems in Europe, Frost and Sullivan, 1987.

Bourdon, R, *The PICK Operating System,* Addison-Wesley, 1986.

Mills, G, Other ways of skinning a cat, *Datalink,* 15th June 1987.

Ireland, S, Neesham, C, Suppliers enter race to develop UNIX interface, *Computing,* 2nd February 1988.

CHAPTER 7

Babcock, C, How faithful will IBM be to UNIX?, *Computer News,* 12th November 1987.

Guest, D, Acid test time, *Datalink,* 25th April 1988.

Powell, M, Praise where praise is due, *Computer Weekly,* 16th July 1987.

CHAPTER 8

The UNIX Systems Marketplace — Western Europe 1986-1992, IDC, 1986.

UNIX Impact on Office Systems, Dataquest, 1987.

Bourdon, R, Pick operating system, *Computing Techniques,* January 1988.

Operating systems' solutions looking for a problem, *Multi-user Computing,* November/December 1987.

Errington, D, Best of both worlds, *UNIX Systems,* March 1988.

UNIX in the UK, Unigram Products, London, 1987.

GENERAL

There is a vast number of books available on virtually all aspects of UNIX. This list is a selection from the range; the computer publishing houses will provide a detailed list on application.

Backhurst, N G, and Davies, P J, *Systems Management under UNIX and UNIX-like Systems,* Sigma Press, 1987.

X/Open Group, *The X/Open Portability Guide,* North-Holland (available from Sarah Burgerhartstraat 25, PO Box 1991, 1000 BZ Amsterdam, The Netherlands).

Haviland, K, Salama, B, *UNIX System Programming,* Addison-Wesley, 1988.

Bourdon, R, *The PICK Operating System — a Practical Guide,* Addison-Wesley, 1987.

Byrne, V, Gillingwater, D, *Attitudes to the Use of Computerised Information Systems for Production Management in Manufacturing Industry,* Sanderson Computers and Loughborough University of Technology, 1987.

CCTA, *Early Experience with Multi-user Office Systems,* IT Series No 7 of Information Technology in the Civil Service, HMSO, 1984.

/usr/group/uk, EUUG and AT&T UNIX Europe Ltd, *The UNIX Systems Products and Services Catalogue,* European edition, Addision-Wesley, (published yearly).

UNIX Products for the Office, NCC Publications (published yearly).

UNIX Product Directory, ix magazine, London, (published yearly — *ix magazine* now absorbed into *Multi-user Computing*).

Ripps, D, *A Guide to Real-time Programming,* ITECH Information Technology Services, 1988.

Kernighan, Pike, *The UNIX Programming Environment,* Prentice Hall, 1984.

Thomas, Rogers, Yates, *Advanced Programmer's Guide to UNIX System V,* Osbourne McGraw-Hill, 1986.

Rosler, L, The Evolution of C, *Bell Labs Technical Journal,* Vol 63, No 8, pp 1685-1699, 1984.

Kernighan, Ritchie, *The C Programming Language,* Prentice Hall, 1988.

Ritchie, Johnson, Lesk, Kernighan, The C Programming Language, *Bell System Technical Journal,* Vol 57, No 6, 1978, pp 1991-2019.

SPECIALIST UNIX PUBLICATIONS

UNIX Systems monthly magazine and *UNIX Yearbook* annual product guide published in association with /usr/group/UK by:

> Eaglehead Publishing Ltd
> 98 Maybury Road
> Woking
> Surrey

CommUNIXations bi-monthly US magazine and *UNIX Products Directory* annual UX product guide published by:

> /usr/group/USA
> Jan Plansky
> 4655 Old Ironside Drive
> 200,
> Santa Clara
> California 95054
> 0101 408 986 8840

Multi-user Computing monthly magazine published by:

> Multi-user Computing
> 42 Colebrooke Row
> London N1 8AF
> 01-704 9351

Publishers of UNIX books

> Addison-Wesley Publishers
> Finchampstead Road
> Wokingham
> Berkshire RG11 2NZ
> 0734 794000

McGraw-Hill Book Co (UK) Ltd
Shoppenhangers Road
Maidenhead
Berkshire RG13 1EY
0628 23432

North-Holland Publishing Co
PO Box 1991
Sara Burgenhartstraat 25
1000 BZ Amsterdam
The Netherlands
010-31-20-5862456

Pitman Publishing
128 Long Acre
London WC2E 9AN
01-379 7383

Prentice Hall
68 Wood Lane End
Hemel Hempstead
Hertfordshire HP2 4RG
0442 231555

Systems Union Ltd
Northampton Lodge
Canonbury Square
London N1 2AN
01-534 3131

Unigram Products
4th Floor
12 Sutton Row
London
W1V 5FH
01-439 1632

UNIX Book Service
35 Bermuda Terrace
Cambridge
CB4 3LD
0223 313273

UNIX and Other Specialist User Groups

Apollo Computers Users Group

Contact: David Elsy

Apollo Computers (UK) Ltd
Aegis Park
Bramley Road
Bletchley
Milton Keynes
Buckinghamshire MK1 1PT
0908 366188

BRS Europe

Contact: L F W Faber

BRS Europe
11 Weymouth Street
London W1Y 1AE
01-580 5271

Business Information Techniques

Contact: Frank Jones

Business Information Techniques
Bradford University Science Park
20-26 Campus Road
Bradford
West Yorkshire BD7 1HR
0274 736766

Databasix

Contact: D Boxhall

Databasix Ltd
Strawberry Hill House
Bath Road
Newbury
Berkshire RG13 1NG
0635 37373

European UNIX Systems User Group
Secretariat

Contact: Helen Gibbons

Owles Hall
Buntingford
Hertfordshire SG9 9PL
0763 73039

Gould Users Group

Contact: Chris Brown

Bristol University
School of Mathematics
University Walk
Bristol BR1 1TW

Hewlett-Packard User Group

Contact: Godfrey Green

ATC Group
13 Courtfield Close
Southbrook
Lincoln LN2 2QN

Informix User Group

Contact: Jeremy Russell

Star Computer Group
Star House
64 Great Eastern Street
London EC2A 3QR
01-739 7633

Pyramid Users Group

Contact: Dr Jame

Rutherford Appleton Laboratory
Chilton Didcot
Oxfordshire OX11 0QX
0235 21900 x 5408

Quadratron Users Association

Contact: Jim Clelland

Yorkshire Television
Television Centre
Leeds LS3 1JS
0532 438283

Shortlands UK User Group

Contact: T E Nicholas

Clyde House
Reform Road
Maidenhead
Berkshire SL6 8BU
0628 75227

Sun UK User Group

Contact: Sue Crozier

Sun House
31-41 Pembroke Broadway
Camberley
Surrey GU15 3XD
0276 62111

/usr/group/USA

Contact: Jan Plansky

4655 Old Ironside Drive
200,
Santa Clara
California 95054
0101 408 986 8840

/usr/group/UK

Contact: Alison Duke

5 Holywell Hill
St Albans
Hertfordshire AL1 1ET
0727 36003

UK UNIX Systems User Group
(EEUG Affiliated)

Contact: Sunil Das

Computer Science Department
The City University
Northampton Square
London EC1
01-252 4399

X/Open Co Ltd

Abbotts House
Abbey Street
Reading
Berkshire RG1 3BD
0734 508311

BSI IST/5/15

Cornelia Boldyreff (Convenor)

Dept of Computer Science
Brunel University
Uxbridge
Middlesex
UB8 3PH

ITUSA UNIX Action Group

R S Walker

ITUSA
Centre Point
103 New Oxford Street
London
WC1A 1DU
01-379 7400

Pick User Group

c/o Allan Pritchard

City of London Polytechnic
139 Minories
London
01-283 1030 x 374

Pick Users Association

c/o Logical Choice (Computer Services) Ltd

3 Newtech Place
66-72 Magdalen Road
Oxford OX4 1RE
0865 727946

Appendix 4
Manufacturers of Hardware

This is by no means a complete list of manufacturers and suppliers of UNIX hardware, merely a sample of the available products. In the same way, details of the type and range of hardware products supplied by each manufacturer represent the situation during the compilation of the book and thus may not accurately reflect the current situation. If there is no range of hardware quoted for a particular manufacturer, this is because no details were at hand prior to publication.

The majority of these companies can also provide a wide range of software for both general office and specific applications. See Appendix 5 'Suppliers of Software', for further providers of software.

ABS Computers
North Street
Portslade
Brighton
Sussex
BN4 1ER
0273 421509
Products supplied: supermini/supermicro

Acer
Grove House
628 London Road
Slough
Berkshire SL3 8QH
0753 686008
Products supplied: PC/supermicro/mini

AES Data (UK) Ltd
AES House
23 Eyot Gardens
Hammersmith
London
W6 9TN
01-741 9033
Products supplied: supermicros/PCs

Alcatel Data Systems
Holbrook House
Cockfosters Road
Barnet
Hertfordshire
EN4 0DU
01-440 4141

Alpha Microsystems GB Ltd
Berkshire House
56 Herschel Street
Slough
Berkshire
SL1 1PY
0753 821922

Altos Computer Systems
Altos House
1 London Road
Hatch Lane
Slough
Berkshire
SL4 3QJ
0753 23024
Products supplied: supermicros/PCs/minis

Amdahl (UK) Ltd
Viking House
19-31 Lampton Road
Hounslow
Middlesex
01-572 7383
Products supplied: mainframes

Andor Systems (UK) Ltd
Genesis Centre, Garrett Field
Science Park South
Birchwood
Warrington
Cheshire
WA3 7BH
0925 828181
Products supplied: supermicros

Apollo Computer (UK) Ltd
Bramley Road
Bletchley
Milton Keynes
MK1 1PT
0908 366188
Products supplied: superminis

Apple Computer UK Ltd
Eastman Way
Hemel Hempstead
Hertfordshire
HP2 7HQ
0442 60244
Products supplied: PCs

Apricot plc
111 Hagley Road
Edgbaston
Birmingham
B16 8LB
021-456 1234
Products supplied: micros

APV Automation Ltd
Fleming Way
Crawley
West Sussex
RH10 2YX
0293 518900
Products supplied: supermicros

Arcaid (Hardware) Ltd
Unit 26
Grove Park
White Waltham
Nr Maidenhead

Berkshire
SL6 3LW
062-882 6564
Products supplied: PCs

Archford Computers International Ltd
3rd Floor
Shirley House
25-27 Camden Road
London
NW1 9LR
01-482 4411
Products supplied: supermicros

Armstrong Micro Electronics
Armstrong House
Heath Road
Darlaston
Wednesbury
West Midlands
WS10 8XL
021-526 3663
Products supplied: PCs

Aston Technology Ltd
Aston Science Park
Love Lane
Birmingham
021-359 4861
Products supplied: supermicros/minis/
   superminis

AT&T UNIX Europe Ltd
International House
Ealing Broadway
London
W5 5DB
01-567 7711

benchMark Technologies
benchMark House
5 Penrhyn Road
Kingston-upon-Thames
Surrey
KT1 2BT
01-541 1944
Products supplied: supermicros/minis

Bleasdale Computer Systems plc
Leicester Road
Lutterworth
Leicestershire
LE17 4HD
0455 556841
Products supplied: supermicros

British Olivetti
154-160 Upper Richmond Road
London SW15
01-789 6699
Products supplied: minis

British Telecom plc
National Networks
1st Floor, Intel House
24 Southwark Bridge Road
London
SE1 9HJ
01-928 8686
Products supplied: supermicros/minis

Cambridge Micro Computers Ltd
Science Park
Cambridge
Cambridgeshire
CB4 4BN
0223 314666
Products supplied: supermicros

CCI
Greyhound House
23/24 George Street
Richmond
Surrey TW9 1JY
01-948 8606
Products supplied: superminis

Compaq Computer Ltd
Ambassador House
Paradise Road
Richmond
Surrey
01-940 8860
Products supplied: PCs

Compass Systems
Bridge House
Faraday Road
Newbury
Berkshire
RG13 2DH
0635 521600
Products supplied: supermicros/suprminis

Compuvision Ltd
Central House
New Street
Basingstoke
Hampshire
RG21 1DP
0256 58133

Concurrent Computer Corp
260A Bath Road
Slough
Berkshire
SL1 4ES
0753 77777

Convergent Solutions Ltd
64 Great Eastern Street
London EC2A 3QR
01-739 7633
Products supplied: minis/superminis

Cray Research (UK) Ltd
London Road
Blackwell
Berkshire
RG12 2SY
0344 485971
Products supplied: mainframes

Crellon Microsystems
3 The Business Centre
Molly Millars Lane
Wokingham
Berkshire
RG11 2EY
0734 788878
Products supplied: minis/micros

Cromenco (UK)
Wordsworth House
PO Box 18
Westerham
Kent
TN16 1EY
0959 63051
Products supplied: supermicros

Cubix Systems Europe
St Peter's House
London End
Beaconsfield
Buckinghamshire
HP9 2JH
04946 78781
Products supplied: supermicros

Data General Ltd
Hounslow House
724-734 London Road
Hounslow
Middlesex
TW3 1PD
01-572 7455
Products supplied: minis/superminis

Data Logic Ltd
Queens House
Greenhill Way
Harrow
Middlesex
HA1 1YR
01-863 0383

Digital Equipment Company Ltd
Queens House
Forbury Road
Reading
Berkshire
RG1 3JH
0734 868711
Products supplied: supermicros/minis/
  superminis

Equinox Computer Systems Ltd
114-116 Curtain Road
London EC2A 3AH
01-739 3450
Products supplied: supermicros

Ferranti Computer Systems Ltd
Simonsway
Manchester
M22 5LA
061-499 6669
Products supplied: supermicros

GEC Ltd
132-135 Long Acre
Covent Garden
London
WC2E 9AH
01-240 7171
Products supplied: supermicros/minis/
  superminis

Gould Electronics
Computer Systems Division
Copthall House
Grove Road
Sutton
Surrey
SM1 1BY
01-643 783631
Products supplied: superminis

Hewlett-Packard Ltd
King Street Lane
Winnersh
Nr Wokingham
Berkshire

RG11 5AR
0734 784774
Products supplied: minis/micros

Honeywell Bull Ltd
Maxted Road
Hemel Hempstead
Hertfordshire
HP2 7DZ
0442 42291

IBM United Kingdom
PO Box 31
Birmingham Road
Warwick
Warwickshire
CV34 5JL
0926 32525
Products supplied: PC/supermicro/mini/
  supermini/mainframe

ICL (UK) Ltd
Bridge House
North Putney Bridge
Fulham
London SW6 3JX
01-788 7272
Products supplied: PCs/supermicros/minis

IMP
Number One Industrial Estate
Medomsley Road
Consett
Co Durham
DH8 6TJ
0207 503481
Products supplied: supermicros

Integrated Solutions
NBI House
462 London Road
Isleworth
Middlesex
TW7 4EP
01-568 8899
Products supplied: supermicros

Intel Corporation (UK) Ltd
Piper's Way
Swindon
Wiltshire
SN3 1RJ
0793 696000
Products supplied: PCs

Intergraph (GB) Ltd
Delta Business Park
Great Western Way
Swindon
Wiltshire
SN5 7XP
0793 619999
Products supplied: supermicros/minis

Interpoint Computer Inc
Grove House
628 London Road
Slough
Berkshire
SL3 8QH
0753 686008
Products supplied: minis

ITL
Technology House
Maylands Avenue
Hemel Hempstead
Hertfordshire
HP2 7DF
0442 42277
Products supplied: supermicros/
    superminis/mainframes

Jarogate Ltd
Unit 7
HQ3
Hook Rise South
Surbiton
Surrey
KT6 7LD
01-391 4433
Products supplied: supermicros

Kode Computers Ltd
Drakes Way
Swindon
SN3 3JL
0793 511345
Products supplied: PCs

LSI Computers
145-157 St John Street
London
EC1V 4QJ
01-250 3535
Products supplied: supermicros

Mannesman Information Systems Ltd
224 Bath Road
Slough

Berkshire
SL1 4DS
0753 33355
Products supplied: supermicros

Mari Advanced Systems Ltd
MARI House
Old Town Hall
Gateshead
Tyne and Wear NE8 1BP
091 490 1515
Products supplied: minis

Masscomp UK Ltd
194 Kings Road
Reading
Berkshire
RG14 5NH
0734 500345
Products supplied: superminis

MIPS Computer Systems Ltd
Mountbatten House
Victoria Street
Windsor
Berkshire
SL4 1HE
0753 857181
Products supplied: supermicros

Modcomp Ltd
The Business Centre
Molly Millar's Lane
Wokingham
Berkshire
RG11 2JO
0734 786808
Products supplied: superminis

Modix Ltd
PO Box 393
Bristol
BS99 7WU
0454 416222
Products supplied: PCs/supermicros

Molecular Computer Ltd
Dorcan House
Meadfield Road
Langley
Slough
Berkshire
SL3 8XD
0753 44113
Products supplied: supermicros

Motorola Computer Systems
27 Market Street
Maidenhead
Berkshire
SL4 1BW
0753 842147
Products supplied: micros/supermicros

NCR Ltd
206 Marylebone Road
London
NW1 6LY
01-725 8242
Products supplied: supermicros

Nixdorf Computer Ltd
125-135 Staines Road
Hounslow
Middlesex
HP2 7BW
0442 217611
Products supplied: supermicros/superminis

Norbain Electronics plc
Norbain House
Boulton Road
Reading
Berkshire
RG2 0LT
0734 752201
Products supplied: micros

Norsk Data Ltd
Benham Valence
Newbury
Berkshire
RG16 8LU
0635 35544
Products supplied: minis

Parallel Computers
45 Ledgers Road
Slough
Berkshire
SL1 1RX
Products supplied: superminis/PCs

PCS Ltd
224 Bath Road
Slough
Berkshire
SL1 4DS
0753 35427
Products supplied: supermicros

Philips Business Systems
Electra House
Bergholt Road
Colchester
Essex
CO4 5BE
0206 575115
Products supplied: minis

Pinnacle Systems plc
Unit 9
Kings Square
Bristol
BS2 8JJ
0272 421014
Products supplied: supermicros

Plessey Microsystems Ltd
Water Lane
Towcester
Northamptonshire
NN12 7JN
0327 50312
Products supplied: micros

Plexus Computers Ltd
16 Cherry Orchard West
Kembrey Park
Swindon
Wiltshire
SN2 6UY
0793 614110
Products supplied: supermicros

Positron Computers Ltd
Unit 16
Deacon Trading Estate
Newton-le-Willows
Lancashire
WA12 9XQ
09252 29741
Products supplied: superminis

Prime Computer (UK) Ltd
Primos House
2-4 Lampton Road
Hounslow
Middlesex
TW3 1JW
01-572 7400
Products supplied: superminis

Pyramid Technology Ltd
Concept 2000
Farnborough Road
Farnborough
Hampshire
GU12 7NA
0252 373035
Products supplied: superminis

Rair Ltd
145-157 St John Street
London
EC1V 4QJ
01-250 3535
Products supplied: supermicros

Sequent Europe Ltd
1 Martindale Road
Hounslow
Middlesex
TW4 7EW
01-570 2066
Products supplied: superminis

Siemens Ltd
St Catherine's House
2 Hanworth Road
Feltham, Middlesex
TW13 5BA
0932 785691
Products supplied: PCs/Supermicros

SK Computer Systems Ltd
St Michael's House
Norton Way South
Letchworth
Herts SG6 1PB
0462 679331
Products supplied: PCs

Sun Microsystems UK Ltd
Sun House
31-41 Pembroke Broadway
Camberley
Surrey
GU15 3XD
0276 62111
Products supplied: micros

Systime Computers Ltd
Leeds Business Park
Morley
Leeds
LS27 0NH
0532 529292
Products supplied: supermicros/minis

Tandem Computers Ltd
Peel House
32-34 Church Road
Northolt
Middlesex
UB5 5AB
01-841 7381

Tandon Computer (UK) Ltd
Unit 19
Dunlop Road
Hunt End
Redditch
Worcester
B97 5XP
0527 46800
Products supplied: PCs

Tandy Corporation
Tandy Centre
Leamore Lane
Bloxwich
Walsall
West Midlands
WS2 7PS
0922 477778
Products supplied: PCs/micros

Televideo Systems International Ltd
Dorna House
50 Guildford Road
West End
Woking
Surrey
GU24 9PW
09905 6464
Products supplied: supermicros/PCs/
   micros

Terminal Display Systems Ltd
Lower Philips Road
Whitebirk Industrial Estate
Blackburn
Lancashire
BB1 5TH
0254 676921
Products supplied: supermicros

Texas Instruments Ltd
Manton Lane
Bedford
MK41 7PA
0234 270111
Products supplied: superminis

Tolerant Systems Ltd
Trident House
15 Bath Road
Slough
Berkshire
SL1 3UJ
0753 691909
Products supplied: supermicros

Torch Computers Ltd
Abberley House
Great Shelford
Cambridge
Cambridgeshire
CB2 5LQ
0223 841000
Products supplied: supermicros

Unisys
Heathrow House
Bath Road
Cranford
Middlesex TW5 9QL
01-750 1400
Products supplied: PCs/supermicros/minis/
   supermini

Unixsys (UK) Ltd
The Genesis Centre, Garrett Field
Science Park South Birchwood
Warrington
Cheshire WA3 7BH
Products supplied: supermicros/minis/
   superminis

Wang (UK) Ltd
Wang House
1000 Great West Road
Brentford
Middlesex TW8 9HL
01-568 9200
Products supplied: supermicros

Wicat Systems Ltd
Wicat House
403 London Road
Camberley
Surrey
0276 686186
Products supplied: supermicros

Zilog (UK) Ltd
Zilog House
43-53 Moorbridge Road
Maidenhead
Berkshire SL6 8PL
0628 39200
Products supplied: supermicros

Appendix 5
Suppliers of Software

This list contains names and addresses of major UK suppliers of software, both authors and retailers. The list is by no means comprehensive, as there are sufficient companies supplying UNIX software to require a substantial directory. Indications are given as to the range and type of software provided by each company; this information is taken from publications and advertisements from April 1987 to May 1988.

This book cannot hope to show the full range of software available from these suppliers or indeed a complete range of suppliers; for this information see the various publications listed in the bibliography.

ACC	=	Accounting	LIB	=	Library
APG	=	Application Generators/4th GLs	MAN	=	Manufacturing
BAC	=	Backup	MED	=	Medical
BES	=	Bespoke	OA	=	Office Automation
BOO	=	Booking System	PAT	=	Patent
CAD	=	CAD/CAM	PAY	=	Payroll
CAER	=	Accident and Emergency Records	PCB	=	Printed Circuit Board Design
COM	=	Communications	PER	=	Personnel
CON	=	Construction	PR	=	Public Relations
DAT	=	Database	PROD	=	Production Control
DIS	=	Distribution	PROJ	=	Project Management
DTP	=	Desktop Publishing	PROP	=	Property Management
EA	=	Estate Agents	PRT	=	Print
ENG	=	Engineering	PUB	=	Publishing
EST	=	Estate Management	REC	=	Recruitment
EXP	=	Expert Systems	RET	=	Retail
FIN	=	Financial	SA	=	School Administration
FLT	=	Fleet Management	SD	=	Software Development
FSS	=	Financial/Spreadsheets	SM	=	Sales and Marketing
GRA	=	Graphics	SS	=	Spreadsheet
HIR	=	Hire	SYS	=	System Software
INS	=	Insurance	RA	=	Travel
INV	=	Investment Management	TRN	=	Training/Education Software
LA	=	Local Authority	WP	=	Word Processing
LEG	=	Legal			

Aarque Systems Ltd
PO Box 70
Blackthorne Road
Colnbrook
Slough
SL3 0AR
Colnbrook 4567

AB Executive (Kingston) Ltd
59 Eden St
Kingston upon Thames
Surrey
KT1 1BW
01-549 6441

Abacus Software Ltd
133 Pall Mall
London
SW1Y 5LU
01-930 4884

ABS Computers
Northe Street, Portslade
Brighton
Sussex
BN4 1DE
0273 421509/LA/PAT/EST/

Abercorn Business Computers Ltd
York House
353A Station Road
Harrow
Middlesex
HA1 1LN
01-861 3727/Turnkey/PROD/ACC/MAN/
OA/FLT/

Abies Informatics Ltd
10 Barley Mow Passage
London
W4 4PH
01-994 6477

Ace Microsystems Ltd
Kew Bridge House
Kew Bridge Road
Brentford
Middlesex
TW8 OEJ
01-847 4673/WP/

Access Technology Ltd
6 Chapel Street
Marlow
Buckinghamshire
SL7 1DD
06284 75517/FSS/

Accounting House Group
Yateley Lodge
Reading Road
Yateley
Camberley
Surrey GU17 7AA
0252 877584/Turnkey/DTP/CON/DIS/FIN/
SD/

Accu-tech Software Service
16 North Street
Rushden
Northants
NN10 9BU
0993 59037

Action File Software
Park Farm House
Heythrop
Chipping Norton
Oxfordshire
OX7 5TW
0608 41197

Adat
Bradford Science Park
1 Campus Rd
Bradford
BD7 1HR
0274 733317

Add-min Computing Ltd
171a High Street
Bromley
Kent
BR1 1NN
01-460 0115

ADP Ltd
Ellerd House
68-72 Stuart Street
Luton
Bedfordshire
LU1 2SW
0582 31271

ADS Computer Engineering Ltd
Unit 1, Ashfield Road
Salisbury
Wiltshire SP2 7EW
0722 338484

AES Data Ltd
AES House
23 Eyot Gardens
Hammersmith
London W6 9TN
01-741 9033

AGS/Systems Strategies
26 Eccleston Square
London
SW1V 1NS
01-931 0005/COM/

AI Computer Corporation
42 Queen St
Maidenhead
Berkshire
SL6 1JE
0628 32516

Aim
Victoria House
Derringham Street
Hull
HU3 1EL
0482 26971

Airline Computer Services
36a High Street
Loughborough, Leics
LE11 2PZ
0509 267616

Alcatel Data Systems
Holbrook House
Cockfosters Road
Barnet
Hertfordshire
EN4 ODU/OA/

AL Downloading Services
166 Portobello Rd
London
W11 2EB
01-727 8722

Alper Systems Ltd
Cambridge Science Park
Milton Road, Cambridge
Cambs CB4 4FQ
0223 862464

Alternative Business Systems Ltd
15a Tamworth St
Lichfield
Staffs
0543 264072

Altos Computer Systems
Altos House
1 London Road
Hatch Lane
Slough
Berkshire
SL4 3QJ
0753 23024/COM/DAT/DTP/FSS/GRA/OA/
SD/

Amac Systems
666 Kenilworth Road
Balsall Common, Nr Coventry
West Midlands CV7 7DY
0676 33707

Amethyst Computer Resource
Unit 9, Workspace 17
Highfield Street, Coalville
Leics LE6 2BR
0530 812458

Amicro Ltd
5 Parklands Parade
Bath Rd, Hounslow West
Middlesex TW5 9AS
01-570 0864

Amplix Services Ltd
Sidehill, Pilgrims Way
Kemsing, Sevenoaks
Kent
0732 61359

Ams Systems & Software Ltd
Concourse House
432 Dewsbury Road
Leeds
LS11 7DF

Amtek Computer Systems
Intersection House
110-120 Birmingham Road
West Bromwich
West Midlands B70 6RX
021-525 8903/Turnkey/HIR/ACC/OA/

Anglia Technology Ltd
Block B
University Village
Wilberforce Road
Norwich NR4 7TJ
0603 503057/Turnkey/ENG/COM/

AP Computer Consultants Ltd
Ascot Road
Holyport Green
Maidenhead
Berkshire SL6 2HY
0628 22428

Apollo Computer (UK) Ltd
Bramley Road
Bletchley
Milton Keynes
MK1 1PT
0908 366188/SD/

Applied Computing Expertise Ltd
1 Sussex Road
New Malden
Surrey
KT3 3PY
01-949 1421

Applied Micros
Applied Micros House
Birchwood Boulevard
Warrington
Cheshire
WA3 7PS
0925 819939

Applied Statistics Research Unit
University of Kent
Canterbury
Kent CT2 7NF
0227 66822

Apricot plc
111 Hagley Road
Edgbaston
Birmingham
B16 8LB
021-456 1234

APT Data Services Unigram
12 Sutton Row
London
W1V 5FH
01-439 1632

APV Automation Ltd
Fleming Way
Crawley
West Sussex
RH10 2YX
0293 518900/Turnkey/MAN/DAT/

Arcadia Computer Services
Lower Ground Floor
36 Colville Terrace
London
W11
01-221 1513/Turnkey/REC/

Arcaid (Hardware) Ltd
Unit 26
Grove Park
White Waltham
Nr Maidenhead
Berkshire
SL6 3LW
062-882 6564/ACC/APG/DAT/OA/SD/

Aregon International Ltd
17 Lincolns Inn Fields
London WC2A 3EG
01-831 7536

Arete Systems Ltd
Nobel House
Greys Road
Henley-on-Thames
Oxfordshire
RG9 1RY
0491 576361/APG/COM/OA/

ASA
Suite 4, Brookland House
46 Kneesworth Street
Royston
Herts SG8 5AQ
0763 47712/CAD/

ASI (UK) Ltd
Carlton House
27a Carlton Drive
Upper Richmond Road
Putney
London
SW15 2TE
01-788 8834

Asset Computer Systems
Burford House
18 Surrenden Crescent
Brighton
East Sussex
BM1 6WF
01-642 6500/Turnkey/CON/REC/ACC/
OA/EA/LEG/

Associated Microsystems
53 East Street
Horsham
West Sussex RH12 1HR
0403 68071

Astech Health Care Systems
35 Dale Street
Manchester
M1 2HF
061-236 1574

Aston Technology Ltd
Aston Science Park
Love Lane
Birmingham
021-359 4861/SD/

AT&T Unix Europe Ltd
International House
Ealing Broadway
London
W5 5DB
01-567 7711/COM/OA/SYS/TRN/WP/

Austec Ltd
Heathcoat House
20 Savile Row, London
W1X 1AE
01-437 9641/SD/

Autodesk Ltd
South Bank Technopark
90 London Road
London
SE1 6LN
01-928 7868/CAD/

Automatic Switching Ltd
Wandle House
Riverside Drive
Mitcham
Surrey CR4 4BU
01-685 9696

Avalon System Ltd
Avalon House
Saffron Road
South Wigston
Leicester
LE8 2TJ
0533 772222/Turnkey/PRT/

Babbage Software Ltd
Victoria House
Victoria St
Totnes
Devon
0803 864328

Basingstoke Technical College
Worting Road
Basingstoke
Hampshire
RG21 1TN
0256 54141

Basmark Europe
32 Broad Street
Wokingham
Berkshire
RG11 1AB
0734 791737/SD/

Basys International Ltd
45 Mortimer St
London
W1V 1PF
01-631 0286

Battelle Software Products Ltd
15 Hanover Square
London
W1R 9AJ
01-409 1443

Beacon Computer Services
Woburn St
Ampthill
Bedford
MK45 2HP
0525 405544

BEC System Services Ltd
Elizabethan House
95 Preston New Road
Blackburn
Lancashire
0254 677215

Bedford Systems Ltd
Phoenix Chambers
15 High Street
Bedford
MK40 1RN
0234 49645/ACC

Bensasson & Chalmers Ltd
6 Kings Parade
Cambridge
Cambs
CB2 1SJ
0223 315733/DAT/

Berkeley Computer Services Ltd
Savoy House
Savoy Centre
Sauchiehall Street
Glasgow
G2 3DH
041-332 0891

Bewley Carlow Computer Systems Ltd
Gerard House
174 Belasis Avenue
Billingham
Cleveland
TS23 1AW
0642 535616/Turnkey/FIN/ACC/

Bivius Systems Ltd
8 High Street
Worthing
West Sussex
BN11 SU2
0903 212481

BLK Business Services Ltd
Archery Road
Eltham
London
SE9 1HA
01-859 6117/Turnkey/DIS/ACC/

Bluebird Systems
21 Hamilton Drive
Glasgow
G12 8DN
041-334 8902/ACC/

Bluetext Ltd
152 Seven Sisters Road
London
N7 7PL
01-272 7337

Blyth Software Ltd
Mitford House
Benhall
Saxmundham
Suffolk
IP17 1JS
0728 3011/APG/

Bolden James Ltd
Dulverton House
Cedar Avenue
Alsager
Stoke-on-Trent
Staffordshire
ST7 2PH
09363 4663/COM/

Bond Associates Ltd
1a Hearne Road
Strand on the Green
Chiswick
London
W4 3NJ
01-994 5534/Turnkey/FIN/LEG/MED/
PUB/REC/DAT/FSS/

Border Business Systems
Sibbersfield Hall
Churton
Chester
Cheshire
0829 270714

Bradford and Ilkely Community College
Dept of Information Technology
Great Horton Road
Bradford
West Yorkshire
BD7 1AY
0274 753309

Brainstorm Computer Solutions
103 Seven Sisters Road
London
N7 7QN
01-281 4411/Turnkey/SD/FSS/

Brainwave Computers Ltd
PO Box 531
Ealing
London
W13 OES
01-833 4901/HIR/

Brandt Communications Ltd
164 Thornton Road
Thornton Heath
Croydon
Surrey
CR4 6BB
01-683 1230

Brazier Computer Systems
8 Valley Rise
Sarisbury Green
Southampton
Hampshire
S03 6BN
04895 3442

Break*through
106 London Street
Reading
Berkshire
RG1 4SJ
0734 391360/ACC/

Brian E Jones
56 Ecclestone Square Mews
London
SW1V 1QN
01-828 4273/SD/

Bridge Software Ltd
Queen Street Chambers
Queen Street
Exeter
Devon
EX4 3RW
0892 410028

Brindley Microcomputers
Unit 2, Cricketts Lane Industrial Estate
Chippenham
Wiltshire
SN15 3EQ
0249 656110

Briter Business Systems
333a Fleet Road
Fleet
Hants
GU13 8BU
0252 620505

British Olivetti
154-160 Upper Richmond Road
London SW15
01-789 6699/COM/DTP/SD/

British Telecom plc
Axion
Martinsham Heath
Ipswich
Suffolk
IP5 7RE
0345 959111/SD/

Britton Lee (Europe) Ltd
71-73 Victoria St
Windsor
Berkshire
SL4 1EY
0753 840900

Brook Street Computers Ltd
The Surrey Research Park
1 Frederick Sanger Road
Guildford
Surrey GU2 5YD
0483 301991/Turnkey/DIS/FIN/MAN/
PROD/

BRS Europe
11 Weymouth St
London
W1N 3FG
01-580 5271/Turnkey/LIB/DAT/

BSS Computer Systems
103-105 New London Road
Chelmsford
Essex
CM2 OPP
0245 269696

Business Computer Projects
St Christopher House
217 Wellington Road South
Stockport
Cheshire
SK2 6PF
061-480 8589/PROP/

Business Computer Support
The Old Cottage
Colmore Lane
Kingwood Common
Henley-on-Thames
Oxfordshire
RG9 1HR
04917 218

Butel Business Systems
Butel House
3 Great West Road
London
W4 5QJ
01-995 1433/ACC/MAN/BOO/

CAD Centre
High Cross
Madingly Road
Cambridge
Cambs
CR3 OHD
0223 314848

Cadlinc Ltd
Highfields Park
University Boulevard
Notts
NG7 2QP
0602 221541

Cadnetix
Cherry Orchard North
Kembrey Park
Swindon
Wiltshire
SN2 6UH
0793 616400/Turnkey/CAD/CAER

Cadsteel Ltd
Bracondale House
141 Buxton Road
Heaviley
Stockport
Cheshire
061-456 8200

Cambridge Graphics Ltd
25 City Rd
Cambridge
Cambridgeshire
CB1 1DP
0223 32361

Cambridge Microcomputers Ltd
Science Park
Milton Road
Cambridge
CB4 4BN
0223 314666

Camdata Systems
71 High Street
Earith
Huntingdon
Cambridgeshire
PE17 3PP
0487 840503

Canbury Systems Ltd
Canbury House
Tolworth Close
Tolworth
Surbiton
Surrey
KT6 7EW
01-399 9248

Carbs International Marketing Ltd
Norman House
Heritage Gate
Derby
DE1 1DD
0332 43255

Care Business Solutions
6 Park Terrace
Worcester Park
Surrey
KT4 7JZ
01-337 7070/Turnkey/SD/APG/

Caxton Print Software
4 Bishops Farm Close
Oakley Green
Windsor
Berkshire
07535 856691

CBSL
Wroughton Place
Cardiff
Wales
CF5 4XB
0222 562255

CCI (Europe) Ltd
49 York Street
Twickenham
Middlesex TW1 3PL
01-892 1122/OA/

Cedardata
66-70 Coombe
New Malden
Surrey
KT3 4QW
01-949 7057

Cemoc Business Computers
1 Samuel Whites
Medina Road
Cowes
Isle of Wight
PO31 7LP
0983 290584

CGRAM Software Ltd
69 Glanbrydan Avenue
Uplands
Swansea
SA2 OHY
0792 474596/Turnkey/MAN/

CGS UK Ltd
Gemini House
133 High Street
Yiewsley
Middlesex
UB7 7QL
0895 444022

Chancelogic plc
Wickham House
Cleveland Way
London
E1 4TR
01-790 2424/APG/

Chancery Data Ltd
15 Bell Street
Reigate
Surrey
RH2 7AD
0474 814929

Chelgraph Ltd
Berkeley Court
High Street
Gloucester
Gloucestershire
GL52 6DA
0242 582442

Chess Consultancies
Sherborne Trading Centre
Unit 6, Sherborne Street
Cheetham Hill
Manchester
061-832 6792

Chris Robinson Consultants
Farmside
Leighton Road
Northall
Bucks
0525 220017

Circulas Ltd
69-73 Theobalds Road
London
WC1
01-242 0223

CIS Computer Services Ltd
49/55 South Street
Dorking
Surrey
RH4 2JX
0306/885507

Clever Connections Ltd
Whitechapel Technical Centre
Unit 2-10
75 Whitechapel Rd
London
E1 1DU
01-247 7467

Clifton-Donkin Ltd
Blagrave House
Blagrave St
Reading
Berkshire
RG1 1PW
0734 596216

Cognita Software Ltd
42 Ewald Road
London
SW6 3ND
01-736 3408/DTP/

Cognosys Ltd
Unit 26
Cherry Orchard North
Kembrey Park
Swindon
Wiltshire
SN2 6UH
0793 619490/EXP/SYS/

Colt Computer Systems
Fairfield Works
Fairfield Road
Hounslow
Middlesex
TW3 1Y
01-577 2686

Columbia Staff & Computers
The Hermitage
45 Church Street
Epsom
Surrey
KT17 4PW
Epsom 28911

Commonsense Computing Ltd
14a Bridgeland Street
Bideford
Devon
EX39 2QE
02372 74795

Communications Public Relations
27 Seabrook Road
Hythe
Kent
CT21 5LX
0303 64753

Compass Systems Ltd
Bridge House
Faraday Road
Newbury
Berkshire
RG13 2DH

Computation Research and
Development Ltd
Devon House
12-15 Dartmouth Street
London
SW1H 9BL
01-222 9822

Computer 7 Business Systems
20b South End
Croydon
Surrey CR0 1DN
01-680 5949

Computer Action Ltd
Central House
27 Park Street
Croydon
Surrey
CR0 1YD
01-686 9777

Computer Answers Ltd
18a Buckingham Avenue
Slough
Berkshire SL1 4QB
0753 76006

Computer Base Ltd
23 Corringway
Ealing
London W5 3AB
01-998 1642/Turnkey/RET//

Computer Consoles (Europe)
Greyhound House
23/24 George Street
Richmond
Surrey
01-948 8607

Computer Factors Ltd
CFL House
Manor Road
Coventry
West Midlands
CV1 2GF
0203 555466

Computer House
172 New Bridge Street
Newcastle-upon-Tyne
NE1 2TE
0632 617001/PAY/FIN/ACC/FSS/

Computer Hyphenation Ltd
17 Avenue Road
St Albans
Hertfordshire
AL1 3QG
0727 52473/DTP/

Computer Methods
25 Station Road
Epping
Essex
CM16 4HH
0378 76894/ACC/

Computer Modelling International
CMI House
8 Chapel Street
Marlow
Bucks
SL7 1DD
06284 75511

Computer Support Associates (UK) Ltd
4 Bridge Street
Caversham
Reading
Berkshire
RG4 8AA
0734 475698/Turnkey/LIB/MED/PER/

Computer Technology Group
Bush House
72 Prince Street
Bristol
Avon
BS1 4HU
0272 290651

Computerline
319 Woodham Lane
Woodham
Weybridge
Surrey KT15 3TB
09323 51022

Computervision Ltd
Central House
New Street
Basingstoke
Hampshire
RG21 1DP
0256 58133/Turnkey/CAD/

Concept Computer Systems Ltd
Bagshot House
37/39 High Street
Bagshot
Surrey GU19 5AF
0276 76303/Turnkey/MAN/

Conosil Systems
100-104 Union Street
Torquay
Devon TQ2 5PY
0803 24311

Conrac UK Ltd
397 Bath Road
Slough
Berkshire
SL1 4ES
06286 65308

Construction Management Computing
Wicor Path
Castle Street
Portchester
Hampshire PO16 9QU
0705 373961/CON/

Contemporary Computation
1-2 Hanover Street
London
W1R 9WB
01-402 5589/Turnkey/DTP/SD/ACC/APG/
DAT/WP/

Context Legal Systems Ltd
Unit 5
Grove Park
White Waltham
Maidenhead
Berkshire
SL6 3LW
062882 6655/LEG/

Control C Software
PO Box 19
Wokingham
Berkshire RG11 2DW
0734 78019

Convergent Technologies (UK) Ltd
Convergent House
Ellesfield Avenue
Southern Industrial Area
Bracknell
Berkshire RG12 4WB
0344 411707/APG/COM/DAT/OA/

Coren Associates Ltd
137-143 High Street
Sutton
Surrey
SM1 1JH
01-642 8010

Cosec Ltd
46-50 Tabernacle St
London
EC2A 4DT
01-253 9922

Cotswold District Council
Computer Services
Trinity Road
Cirencester
Gloucestershire
GL7 1PX
0285 5757/LA/

Counterpoint
5 Blythswood Court
Anderston Cross Centre
Glasgow
Scotland G2 7PH
041 248 5544

CP Computer Services
The Old Rectory
46 Leicester Road
Narborough
Leicester
LE9 5DF
0533 867510/Turnkey/DIS/MAN/

CPT (UK) Ltd
Mitre House
155 Staines Road
Hounslow
Middlesex
TW3 3JQ
01-570 3636/APG/COM/DAT/OA/WP/

CQS
27b Bell Street
Reigate
Surrey RH2 7AD
073 72 22249

CRA Software Ltd
127 Cambridge Science Park
Milton Road
Cambridge
CB4 4GD
0223 862668

Culloville Ltd
Parkview House
81 Springfield Road
Chelmsford
Essex CM2 6JL
0245 359577

D Kipping Ltd
The Systems Centre
Chester Street
Chestergate
Stockport
Cheshire SK3 OB
061-477 3880/Turnkey/LEG/

D M England & Partners
Lytham Court
Lytham
Woodley
Reading
Berkshire RG5 3PQ
0734 699777

Daemon Software
34 Princess Road West
Leicester
LE1 6TJ
0533 557921

Daman Ltd
Barkan House
475 Bolton Road
Pendlebury
Manchester M27
061-793 7015

Dashco
24 Terenure Road
East Rathgar
Dublin 6
Ireland
Dublin 961206

Data Command Ltd
91 Regents Park Road
London
NW1 8UR
01-586 5882

Data Processing Network Ltd
6 Mount Pleasant
Douglas
Isle of Man
0624 20557

Data Systems (Software) Ltd
Woodrow House
78-84 Warrent Road
Woodingdean
Brighton
Sussex BN2 6BA
0273 606402/Turnkey/DIS/ACC/

Database Experts
1 Thames Avenue
Windsor
Berkshire SL4 1QP
0753 840197

Databasix Ltd
Strawberry Hill House
Bath Road
Newbury
Berkshire
RG13 1NG
0635 37373

Datacode Systems (International) Ltd
1-2 Leeson Close
Dublin 2
Ireland
Dublin 688481

Dataflex Services Ltd
16 Anning Street
New Inn Yard
London EC2A 3HB
01-729 4460

Dataflow Ltd
Unit 18
Central Trading Estate
Staines
Middlesex
0784 54171

DataGuild Ltd
Unit 9
The Pines Trading Estate
Broad Street
Guildford
Surrey
GU3 3BH
0483 574463/COM/

Datamode (educom) Ltd
Rodary House
Alderton Crescent
London NW4 3XX
01-202 2664/Turnkey/DIS/MAN/PROD/
PUB/

Datasolve Ltd
4th Floor
Glen House
Stag Place
London
SW1E 5AG
01-828 7878

Datavision (UK) Ltd
121 Talbot Road
Blackpool
Lancashire
FY1 3TA
0253 21444/SD/

Dataware Ltd
Woodley Park Estate
Reading Road
Woodley
Near Reading
Berkshire
RG5 3AW
0734 699688/CAD/

Daton System Ltd
140 High Street
Wootton Bassett
Swindon
Wiltshire
SN4 7AY
0793 854606

David Brew & Associates
9 The Square
Hillsborough
Co Down
Northern Ireland
BT26 6AG
0846 683575

David Dillingstone Systems
158 Victoria Street
London
SW1E 5LB
01-630 6248

Davies & Brown Computer Systems Ltd
9 Boundary Road
Hove
East Sussex
BN3 4EH
0273 424621

Davy Computing
Moorfoot House
2 Clarence Lane
Sheffield S3 7UZ
0742 761201

Deductive Systems Ltd
Brunel Science Park
Kinston Lane
Uxbridge
Middlesex
UB8 3PQ
0895 73505/EXP/

Deecal International
Nagor House
Dundrum Road
Windy Arbour
Dublin 14
0001 988555/COM/

Definitive Computing Ltd
Unit 17
Premier Partnership Estate
The Leys
Brockmoor
Brierley Hill
West Midlands
0384 261727/Turnkey/CON/ACC/

Denford Machine Tools Ltd
Birds Royd
Brighouse
West Yorkshire HD6 1NB
0484 712264

Des Cullen Software
Carrickfree
Glencormac
Kilmacanogue
Co Wicklow
Ireland
Co Wicklow 8675

Dextrafile Ltd
Guardian House
42 Preston New Road
Preston
Lancashire
BB2 6AH
0254 691235/Turnkey/DTP/DIS/PROD/
ACC/

Dialogic Computer Consultants
53 Newbiggen Street
Thaxted
Essex
CM6 2QS
0371 830388

Digitab
1b Harewood Row
London
NW1 6SE
01-258 1919

Digita International Ltd
Kelsey House
Barns Road
Budleigh Salterton
Devon
EX9 6HJ
03954 5059/DAT/

Digital Business Systems Ltd
Digital House
Michigan Avenue
Off Broadway
Salford
M5 2GL
061-872 1495

Digital Equipment Company Ltd
Queens House
Forbury Road
Reading
Berkshire
RG1 3JH
0734 868711/COM/SD/

Digitus Ltd
16-17 Clerkenwell Close
London
EC1R OAA
01-251 1010/Turnkey/SD/ACC/APG/COM/
DAT/OA/SYS/TRN/

Dillon Technology
McGraw-Hill House
Shoppenhangers Road
Maidenhead
Berkshire RG13 1EY
0628 75751

Doctor Dos Ltd
Blagrove House
2-3 Newport Street
Old Town
Swindon
Wiltshire
SN1 3DZ
0793 618458/Turnkey/CAD/FIN/DTP/SS/
DAT/SD/

Donoghue Information Systems
Shenstone Drive
Aldridge
Walsall
West Midlands
WS9 8TP
0222 52803

Doric Computer Systems
23 Woodford Road
Watford
Hertfordshire
WD1 1PB
0923 52288

DSR plc
266-270 Regent Street
Oxford Circus
London
W1R 5DA
01-439 7622

DTA Computer Systems Ltd
70 Claremount Road
Surbiton
Surrey
KT6 4RH
01-390 4681/COM/DAT/

Dyadic Systems Ltd
Park House
The High Street
Alton
Hampshire
GU34 1EN
0420 87024/Turnkey/SD/APG/

Eastern Data Processing Ltd
Whitelands
Hatfield Peverel
Chelmsford
Essex
CM3 2AG
0245 380009/Turnkey/DIS/SD/

Eastman-Stuart Ltd
30 Clarendon Road
Watford
Hertfordshire
WD1 1JJ
0923 55050/ACC/

Elex
John Scott House
Market Street
Bracknell
Berkshire
RG12 1JB
0344 52929

Ellis Associates
379c Fulham Palace Road
London
SW6 6TA
01-384 1057

Elxsi
Ensign House
Brighton Road
Addlestone
Surrey
KT15 1PU
0932 57729

Enterprise Systems Group
Thameside Computer Centre
Summer Road
Thames Ditton
Surrey
KT7 0QJ
01-398 8511

EPS Consultants
Boundary House
Boston Road
London
W7 2QE
01-439 8221

Equinox Computer Systems Ltd
114-116 Curtain Road
London
EC2A 3AH
01-739 3450/ACC/

Estimation Ltd
Highland Road
Shirley
Solihull
West Midlands
B90 4NL
021-704 3221

European Computing
57 West End Avenue
Harrogate
West Yorkshire
HG2 9BX
0423 509350/APG/

Europel Systems Ltd
5 Vo-Tec Centre
Hambridge Lane
Newbury
Berkshire
RG14 5TN
0635 31074/GRA/

Evets Computers Ltd
123-125 Green Lane
Derby
DE1 1RZ
Derby 363981

Excelan
Weir Bank
Bray-on-Thames
Nr Maidenhead
Berkshire
SL6 2ED
0628 34281/COM/

Farmdata Ltd
Westertown
Rothienorman
Aberdeen
AB5 8US
04675 457/ACC/

Fastnet Systems
Fastnet House
73 Long Lane
London
EC1A 9ET
01-606 3044/Turnkey/FIN/ACC/

FCMC plc
46 Chagford Street
London
NW1 6EB
01-262 1021/OA/

FDS Microsystems Ltd
76-80 City Road
London
EC1Y 2ES
01-251 8866

Feilden & Mawson
Ferry Road
Norwich
Norfolk
NR1 1SU
0603 629571

Ferrari Software Ltd
Ferrari House
Church Road
Egham
Surrey
TW20 9LB
0784 38900

Ffoss Ltd
1 St John Estate
Tylers Green
Penn
High Wycombe
Buckinghamshire
HP10 8HR
049 481 6669

Figure Flow Ltd
9 Market Place
Hadleigh
Suffolk IP7 5DL
0473 822917

Focus Software Consultants
95 Beverly Road
Hull
North Humberside
HU3 1XY
0482 28120/APG/CAD/OA/

Foresight Systems
St Annes House
St Annes Road
Bristol
Avon BS4 4AD
0272 719506

Foxgrove Software Ltd
6 Westow Hill
Upper Norwood
London
SE19 1RX
01-761 7823

Fraser Williams (Southern) Ltd
Landseer House
19 Charing Cross Road
London
WC2H OES
01-839 5451/Turnkey/SD/ACC/

Fretwell-Downing Data Systems
5 Onslow Road
Sheffield
South Yorkshire
S11 7AE
0742 682301

G + G Software
31 High Cross Street
St Austell
Cornwall
PL25 4AN
0726 68800

Gateway Business Systems
6 Station Road
New Milton
Hants
BH25 6JU
0425 616843

GEC Software Ltd
132 Long Acre
London
WC2E 9AH
01-240 7171/COM/SD/

General Robotics European Sales Ltd
2nd Floor
Grove House
551 London Road
Isleworth
Middlesex
TW7 4DS
031 2256934

Genus Systems Ltd
9a St Colme Street
Edinburgh
Lothian
EH3 6AA
031-22556934/DAT/SD/SYS/

Glockenspiel Ltd
19 Belvedere Place
Dublin 1
Republic of Ireland
0001 73 51 59

Goldcrest Computer Systems
10 Tower Crescent
Neath Hill
Milton Keynes
Bucks
MK14 6JY
0908 676198/Turnkey/DIS/FIN/MAN/
PROD/RET/SD/

Golden Gate Ltd
Winchester House
Gardner Road
Maidenhead
Berkshire
SL6 7RL
0628 783631/Turnkey/DTP/

Gordon & Gotch Computers
Walton House
Central Trading Estate
Staines
Middlesex
TW18 4UX
0784 62401

Gould Computer Systems
Copthall House
Grove Road
Sutton
Surrey
SM1 1BY
01-643 8020

Grab IT Ltd
29 Chartwell Drive
Wigston
Leicester
Leics
0533 811999

Graffcom Systems Ltd
CP House
97-107 Uxbridge Road
Ealing
London
W5 5TL
01-579 9407

Graham Smith
4 Chatsworth Road
Cheam
Surrey
SM3 K8PJ
01-641 0276

Gresham Business Computers Ltd
22-27a St Mary Street
Southampton
Hampshire
SO1 1NP
0703 39719/Turnkey/FIN/APG/

Grove Systems Ltd
3 Ashlyn Grove
Fallowfield
Manchester
M14 6YD
061 224 4465

GST Professional Services
8 Green Street
Willingham
Cambridge
Cambridgeshire
CB4 5JA
0954 61244

H Walton Technical Systems
17 Barton Street
Bath
Avon
BA1 1HQ
0225 62601

Hall Associates (UK) Ltd
Sandhursy House
297 Yorktown Road
Camberley
Surrey
GU15 4QA

Harris Baldry Consultants
101a Clapham High Street
London
SW4 7TB
01-622 2445/Turnkey/CON/

Harvest Solutions Ltd
Harvest House
Paddock Road
Caversham
Reading
Berkshire RG4 OBY
0734 474766

HCL Systems Ltd
21 High Street
Sandy
Bedfordshire
SG19 1AG
0767 292111/ACC/

HCR UK
PO Box 156
Marlborough
Wiltshire
SN8 1JS
0672 55582

Heldya Software Ltd
Unit 7
6 Pardown
Oakley
Basingstoke
Hampshire RG23 7DY
0256 782313/Turnkey/FIN/ACC/MAN/

Helpware
39 Cinderhill Lane
Sheffield
South Yorkshire
S8 8JA
0742 784774

Hewlett-Packard Ltd
King Street Lane
Winnersh
Nr Wokingham
Berkshire
RG11 5AR
0734 696622/CAD/SD/

Hexagon
Avenue Four
Station Lane
Witney
Oxfordshire
OX3 7BN
0993 74591/PROP/

High Level Hardware Ltd
PO Box 170
Windmill Road
Headington
Oxford
OX3 7BN
0865 750494

Highbrave Ltd
78 Cannon Lane
Pinner
Middlesex
HA5 1HR
01-429 0370

Hi-Tek Solutions
Ditton Walk
Cambridge
CB5 8QD
0223 213535/ACC/DAT/OA/

Honeywell Bull Ltd
Maxted Road
Hemel Hempstead
Hertfordshire
HP2 7DZ
0442 42291/ACC/APG/COM/DAT/OA/SD/

Honeywood Software Ltd
6b Middle Street
Yeovil
Somerset
BA20 1LZ
0935 71117

Horizon Software Ltd
27 East Street
Leicester
LE1 6NB
0533 556550

HRC Micro Organisation
1 Hereford Street
Sheffield
S1 4PR
0742 755047

Human Computing Resources
Richmond House
Bath Road
Speen
Newbury
Berks
RG13 1QY

Hytech Consultants
Chequers Parade
Wycombe Road
Prestwood
Bucks
HA6 OPN
02406 6071

Hytec Microsystems Ltd
33 Witney Road
Eynshawe
Oxfordshire
OX8 1QD
0865 882955/Turnkey/SA/CAER/FLT/

IA Datasystems
Croft House
11 Bancroft
Hitchin
Herts
SG5 1JOP
0462 57141/Turnkey/FIN/

IBM (UK) Ltd
PO Box 116
Northern Cross
Basingstoke
Hampshire
RG21 1EJ
0256 56144/CAD/

IBR Information Systems
2 The Western Centre
Western Road
Bracknell
Berkshire
RG12 1RW
0344 486555

Icaps Ltd
The Old Surgery
Dr Middletons Road
Chalford Hill
Stroud
Gloucester GL6 8NQ
0453 885554/ACC/PROD/

ICL (UK) Ltd
Infopoint
Bridge House North
Putney Bridge
Fulham
London SW6 3JX
01-788 7272/APG/CAD/DAT/MAN/
OA/SD/

ICS Computing Ltd
Queens Road
Belfast
Northern Ireland
BT3 9DT
0232 54166

Icus Ireland Ltd
31 Adelaide Road
Dublin 2
0001 785899/ACC/APG/COM/DAT/FSS/
OA/SYS/WP/

ILA Computer Systems Ltd
5a Heath Hurst Road
Hampstead
London
NW3 2RU
01-435 4275

Imtec Group plc
170 Honeypot Lane
Stanmore
Middlesex
HA7 1LB
01-204 3456

Infodata Systems Ltd
Mill Reef House
9-14 Cheap Street
Newbury
Berkshire
RG14 5DD
0635 32741

Infomatrix Ltd
4 Eldon Square
Newcastle-upon-Tyne
Tyne and Wear
NE1 7JG
0632 328044

Information Design Consultants
Bristol House
Victoria House
Bristol
Avon
BS1 6BY
0272 276140/SD/

Information Engineering Software Ltd
The Green
Northmoor
Oxfordshire
OX8 1SX
086 731 740/APG/SD/

Information Technology plc
Technology House
Maylands Avenue
Hemel Hempstead
Herts HP2 7DF
0442 42277/APG/OA/TRN/

Innovative Software
Southampton House
192-206 York Road
London
SW11 35A
01-223 3876/OA/

Intasoft Ltd
60 Portland St
Exeter
Devon
EX1 2EQ
0392 21760/SD/

Integrated Micro Products Ltd
Number One Industrial Estate
Medomsley Road
Consett
Co Durham
DH8 6TJ
0207 503481

Integrated Solutions
462 London Road
Isleworth
Middlesex
TW7 4EP
01-568 4242/Turnkey/DTP/SD/

Intektra Data UK
Chapel Lane
Stockton Heath
Warrington
Cheshire
WA4 6LL
0925 602693

Intelligence Ireland
Nagor House
Dundrum Road
Windy Arbour
Dublin 14
Ireland
Dublin 988555

Intelligent Terminals Ltd
George House
36 North Hanover
Glasgow
Strathclyde
G1 2AD
041-552 1353

Intercon Computers Ltd
Southbank House
Black Prince Road
London
SE1 7SJ
01 583 9982/3

Intergraph (GB) Ltd
Delta Business Park
Great Western Way
Swindon
Wiltshire
SN5 7XP
0793 619999/CAD/

International Business Software
Coworth Park House
Coworth
Ascot
Berkshire
SL5 7SF
0990 28841

Interphase International Inc
93a New St
Aylesbury
Buckinghamshire
HP20 2NY
0296 435661

Interwaste
40 The Avenue
Roundhay
Leeds
Yorkshire
LS8 1JG
0532 661885

ITECH
Science Park
University of Warwick
Coventry
CV4 7EZ
0203 414357

ITL
Technology House
Maylands Avenue
Hemel Hempstead
Hertfordshire
HP2 7DF
0442 42277/DAT/

ITT/ESC
PO Box 39
Harlow
Essex
CM20 2SY
0279 27822

James Findlay & Associates
21 Bramble Bank
Grimley Green
Camberley
Surrey
GU16 6PN
0252 836450

Jared and Associates Ltd
Southbank House
Black Prince Road
London
SE1 7SJ
01-582 4250

Jaro Marketing Ltd
Bank House
1-7 Sutton Court Road
Sutton
Surrey
SM1 4SZ
01-642 6500

Jayswood Systems Ltd
Colonial Way
Watford
Herts
WD2 4AW
0923 31048

John Rutherford & Partners
Bell House
Copthorne Bank
Copthorne
West Sussex
RH10 3JD
0342 712889

JSB Computer Systems
Cheshire House
Castle St
Macclesfield
Cheshire
SK11 6AF
0625 33618/SYS/

JV Consultants Ltd
4 Loughborough Road
Mountsorrel
Leics
LE12 7AT
0533 302880

K A Spencer (Software)
74 Dovers Park
Bathford
Nr Bath
Avon BA1 7VE
0225 858464

K & H Project Systems
Felco House
72A Richmond Road
Kingston on Thames
Surrey
KT2 5EL
01-549 0056/Turnkey/PROJ/

Kalamazoo plc
Mill Lane
Northfield
Birmingham
B31 2RW
021-475 2191/ACC/APG/

KCS Management Systems
Whitecliff House
852 Brighton Road
Purley
Surrey
CR2 2UY
01-660 2444/FSS/PAY/

Keen Computers
Minerva House
Spaniel Row
Nottingham
NG1 6EP
0602 412777

Keith Brindle Associates Ltd
263 Frimley Green
Camberley
Surrey
GU16 6LD
0252 837231

Kent Barlow Information Associates
250 Kings Road
Chelsea
London
SW3 5UE
01-351 2776

Kernel Technology Ltd
21 Queen St
Leeds
South Yorkshire
LS21 2TW
0532 465311/EXP/SD/

Kerridge Computer Co Ltd
c/o VP Ltd
7 Links Way
London NW4 1JR
01-203 4685

Kewill Systems Ltd
Ashley House
20-32 Church St
Walton-on-Thames
Surrey
0932 248328

KM Computing Ltd
Wirral Business Centre
Gorsey Lane
Dock Road
Birkenhead
Wirral
L41 1JW
051-630 1020/Turnkey/DTP/LEG/ACC/
APG/DAT/FSS/OA/WP/

Knowledge Base Services Ltd
Campus Road
Listerhills Technology Park
Bradford
West Yorks
BD7 1HR
0274 736895

Kodak Ltd
Kodak House
PO Box 66
Station Road
Hemel Hempstead
Herts
HP1 1JU
0442 61122

KPG Computer Systems Ltd
The Baltic Centre
Great West Road
Brentford
Middlesex
TW8 9BU
01-568 4633

Law Data Systems Ltd
Bridge House
Westgate
Leeds LS1 4ND
0532 462841/LEG/

LDR Systems Ltd
Victoria House
Aldershot
Hants
GU11 1EJ
0252 331666

Legal Support Services Ltd
St James House
East St
Farnham
Surrey
GU9 7SR
0252 723555/LEG//

Level V Distribution Ltd
Ashford House
Dale Road South
Matlock
Derbyshire
DE4 3DB
0629 733141/DAT/FSS/OA/SYS/WP/

Lex Systems Leasing Ltd
Lex House
Stonefield Way
South Ruislip
Middlesex
HA4 OLA
01-845 5544/Turnkey/FIN/RET/ACC/DAT/
DTP/OA/WP/

Life Insurance Network Software
Pine Cottage
Paddocks Way
Ashtead
Surrey
KT21 2QY
Ashtead 78676

Lmr Computer Services
54-70 Moorbridge Road
Maidenhead
Berkshire
SL6 8BN
0628 37123

Logica International Ltd
64 Newman Street
London
W1A 4SE
01-637 9111

Logical Business Systems
Genesis Centre
Birchwood Science Park
Risley
Warrington
Cheshire WA3 7BH
0925 824660

Logical Choice
3 Newtec Place
Magdalen Road
Oxfordshire
OX4 1RE
0865 727946/DAT/

Logic Based Systems Ltd
40 Beaumont Avenue
Richmond
Surrey
TW9 2HE
01-940 9563

Logic Programming Associates Ltd
Studio 4
Royal Victoria Patriotic Building
Trinity Road
London
SW18 3SX
01-871 2016

Logic Replacement Technology Ltd
6 Arkwright Road
Reading
Berkshire
RG2 OLS
0734 751087

Logitek plc
Logitek House
Bradley Lane,
Standish
Greater Manchester
WN6 OXQ
0257 426644/OA/

Logsys (Advanced Systems) Ltd
Logsys House
Ashville Way
Wokingham
Berkshire
RG11 2PL
0734 794121/Turnkey/SD/

M2S/Modix Ltd
Unit No 12
King Square
Bristol
BS2 8JJ
0272 425573/Turnkey/SD/

M2 Systems Ltd
Simonsway
Wythenshawe
Manchester
M22 5LA
061-499 3355/SYS/

Magnasys Ltd
10 Ainsdale Road
Ealing
London
W5 1JX
01-997 9916/SD/

Magstore Ltd
PO Box 121
Erith
Kent
DA8 1SR
0322 339922

Mai UK Ltd
Black Arrow House
Chandos Road
London
NW10 6NF
01-965 9731/OA/

Management Coordinations Ltd
Wilmslow House
Water Lane
Wilmslow
Cheshire SK9 5AG
0625 532865

Mannesman Information Systems Ltd
224 Bath Road
Slough
Berkshire
SL1 4DS
0753 33355/Turnkey/CON/LEG/MAN/SD/

Manufacturing Management Ltd
Refuge House
2-4 Henry Street
Bath
Avon BA1 1JT
0225 60473/CAD/MAN/

Map Computer Systems
7 Blythswood Court
Anderston Cross Centre
Glasgow
041-204 0811

Mark Harrison (Systems
& Technology) Ltd
8 Mayflower Close
Chineham
Basingstoke
Hampshire
RG24 OXS
0256 63914

MARI Advanced Microelectronics
MARI House
Old Town Hall
Gateshead
Tyne & Wear
NE8 1BR
091-490 1515

MASS Ltd
15 Grampian Court
Almondvale Centre
Livingston
EH54 6QF
0506 412362/DAT/SYS/

Matrix Resource Management
Matrix House
Goodman Street
Leeds
West Yorkshire
LS10 1PA
0532 444722

MBS Microtex Ltd
Unit 6
Kings Ride Park
Ascot, Berks
SL5 8BP
0990 28051

McDowell Knaggs & Associates
Shades House
Mealcheapen St
Worcester
Worcs
0905 612266

McGrane Computer Systems
36 Lad Lane
Dublin 2
Ireland
Dublin 612010

McGraw-Hill Book Co (UK) Ltd
Shoppenhangers Road
Maidenhead
Berkshire
SL6 2QL
0628 23432

McGuffie Brunton Ltd
The Granary
50 Barton Road
Worsley
Manchester
061-793 1175

MD/8
35 Upland Road
South Croydon
Surrey
CP2 6EE
01-688 5794

Medical Computer Services Ltd
5 The Pentangle
Park St
Newbury
Berkshire
RG13 1EU
0635 36655/Turnkey/MED/

Medixsys Ltd
The Genesis Centre, Garrett Field
Science Park South Birchwood
Warrington
Cheshire WA3 7BH
0925 828181/Turnkey/MED/

Medoc Computers Ltd
Trivett House
1 Short Hill
Nottingham
Notts
NG1 1HY
0602 582438

MEM Computer Systems Ltd
9 Woburn Street
Ampthill
Beds
MK45 2HP
0525 404262

Memory Computer plc
31 Adelaine Road
Dublin 2
0001 785899/Turnkey/SD/ACC/

Mentor Systems plc
Refuge Assurance Buildings
Ainsworth St
Blackburn
Lancashire
BB1 6AZ
0254 675511/ACC/

Mercia Software Ltd
Aston Science Park
Love Lane
Birmingham
West Midlands
B7 4BJ
021-359 5096

Mertec Computer Products
35-36 Singleton Street
Swansea
West Glamorgan
SA1 3QN
0792 467980

Metacomco
26 Portland Square
Bristol
Avon
BS2 8RZ
0272 428781

Metascybe Systems Ltd
Grant House
47-53 St John St
London
EC1M 4AN
01-253 1001/COM/

MFT Computer Systems Ltd
MFT House
North Parkway
Seacroft
Leeds
LS14 6PX
0532 738244/Turnkey/OA/PROP/DAT/OA/

MGA Microsystems
140 High Street
Tenterden
Kent
TN30 6HT
05806 4278

MGB Computer Services
(South East Region)
Hamilton House
111 Marlowes
Hemel Hempstead
Herts HP1 1BB
0442 212511/ACC/

Microapl Ltd
Unit 1F, Nine Elms Industrial Estate
87 Kirtling Street
London
SW8 5BP
01-662 0395

Microbel Ltd
The Loft
Lord Nelson Yard
Sutton-on-Trent
Newark
Nottinghamshire
NG23 6PF
0636 821722/MAN/

Microdrive Systems Ltd
Virginia Villas
High St
Hartley Wintney
Hampshire
RG27 8NR
025126 4646/Turnkey/FIN/BES/ACC/

Micro Focus
26 West Street
Newbury
Berkshire
RG13 1JT
0635 32646/APG/SD/SYS/

Microft Technology Ltd
The Old Powerhouse
Kew Gardens Station
Kew
Surrey TW9 3PS
01-948 8255/DAT/

Microman Ltd
St Johns Innovation Centre
Cowley Road
Cambridgeshire
CB4 4WS
0223 341130/MAN/

Micromaster Software Ltd
Rockingham House
Broad Lane
Sheffield
S Yorkshire
S1 4BS
0742 755134

Microprocessor Application Group
Cranfield Institute of Technology
Cranfield
Bedfordshire
MK43 OAL
0234 752704

Microprocessor Developments Ltd
3 Canfield Place
London
NW6 3BT
01-328 2277/APG/

Microsoft Europe
Excel House
49 Demonfort Road
Reading
Berkshire
RG1 8LP
0734 500741

Microspecific Ltd
Unit 3
Pillings Road Industrial Estate
Oakham
Rutland
Leics
0572 2528

Midas Advisory Services
23 St Martins Street
Wallingford
Oxfordshire
OX10 36773

Midshires Computers
Mirion House
Earle St
Crewe
Cheshire
CW1 2AS
0270 589191/REC/SYS/

Mills Microsoftware
Wonastow Road
Monmouth
Gwent
NP5 3AH
0600 5831

Minnie Business Systems
65 London Wall
London
EC2M 5YU
01-638 3815

Mitsubishi Electric UK Ltd
Hertford Place
Denham Way
Maple Cross
Rickmansworth
Herts
0923 770000

MML Ltd
Refuge House
2-4 Henry St
Bath
Avon
BA1 1JT
0225 60473

Modcomp Ltd
The Business Centre
Molly Millars Lane
Wokingham
Berkshire
RG11 2JO
0734 786808/COM/MAN/

Modern Business Technology Ltd
PO Box 87
Guildford
Surrey
GU4 8BB
04868 23956/SD/

Modula-Software Ltd
29 Alma Vale Road
Clifton
Bristol
Avon
BS8 2HL
0272 742796

MS Associates Ltd
Castle Chambers
3-9 Sheet St
Windsor
Berks
0753 842147/SYS/

Multi Concepts
32 Broad Street
Wokingham
Berkshire
RG11 1AB
0734 791737/MAN/

Multisoft Systems Ltd
Cross & Pillory House
Cross & Pillory Lane
Alton
Hampshire
GU34 1HL
0420 85572

NAG (Numerical Algorithms Group) Ltd
Mayfield House
256 Banbury Road
Oxford
Oxfordshire
OX2 7DE
0685 511245/SD/

NCR Ltd
206 Marylebone Road
London
NW1 6LY
01-725 8242/ACC/APG/CAD/MAN/

Nixdorf Computer Ltd
125-135 Staines Road
Hounslow
Middlesex
HP2 7BW
0442 217611
/Turnkey/ENG/CAD/FIN/MAN/PROD/
APG/CAD/DAT/EXP/

Norbain Electronics plc
Norbain House
Boulton Road
Reading
Berkshire
RG2 0LT
0734 752201/APG/

Northern Telecom plc
Maylands Avenue
Hemel Hempstead
Herts HP2 7LD
0442 41141/OA

Offline Systems Ltd
40 Queen Street
Edinburgh
EH2 3NH
031-225 4542

OI Computers
Southampton House
192-206 York Road
London
SW11 3SA
01-228 2207

Olympic Computers
241 Oxford Road
Reading
Berkshire
RG1 7PX
0734 507457

Optichrome Computer Systems Ltd
Maybury Road
Woking
Surrey
GU21 5HX
04862 27661/Turnkey/PRT//

Optim Computer Group
Optim House
Blackhorse Road
Letchworth
Herts
SG6 1HT
04626 70661

Oracle Corporation UK Ltd
Thames Link House
1 Church Road
Richmond
Surrey
TW9 2QE
01-948 6911/DAT/

Oriel Computers Ltd
1-5 West Street
Chipping Norton
Oxon
OX7 5LY
0608 41351/4

Output Software Ltd
Unit 151
Cannon Workshops
3 Cannon Drive
London
E14 9SA
01-987 2224/COM/

PA Manufacturing Services
Cambridge Laboratory
Melbourn
Royston
Hertfordshire
SG8 6DP
0763 61222

Package Programs of London
91 Blackfriars Road
London SE1 8HW
01-633 0121

Panacea Ltd
Winton House
Winton Square
Winchester Road
Basingstoke
Hampshire
RG21 1EN
0256 840458
/Turnkey/DIS/FIN/ENG/HIR/MAN/SM/
TRA/ACC/APG/COM/DAT/OA/SD/WP/

Paragon Technology International
Mountbatten House
Victoria St
Windsor
Berkshire
SL4 1HE
0753 557181

Parsoft Ltd
Berkeley House
51-53 High Street
Redhill
Surrey
RH1 1RX
0737 764500/APG/

Paxton Computers
28 New Street
St Neots
Cambs
PE19 1AJ
0480 217777/ACC/

PC Support Ltd
5-7 Forlease Road
Maidenhead
Berkshire
SL6 1RP
0628 75579

Pennine Computer Company Ltd
Office Park 41
Dean Clough
Halifax
West Yorkshire
HX3 5AX
0422 41719

Pentagon Business Systems plc
42-50 Hersham Road
Walton-on-Thames
Surrey
KT12 1RQ
0932 246601/ACC/OA/

Perception Software System
London House
243-253 Lower Mortlake Road
Richmond
Surrey
TW9 2LL
0272 217040

Perrin Systems Ltd
Whaley Road
Barugh Green
Barnsley
West Yorkshire
S75 1HT
0226 731111/Turnkey/T/CAD/ENG/CAD/

Perspective Design Ltd
9 Pembroke Street
Cambridge
CB2 3QY
0223 323636

Philips Business Systems
Electra House
Berholt Road
Colchester
Essex CO4 5BE
0206 575115

Pierce Management Services
Dickenson House
30 Albion Street
Chipping Norton
Oxfordshire OX7 5BJ
0608 41901/EST/

Pinpoint Analysis Ltd
Mercury House
117 Waterloo Road
London SE1 8UL
01-928 1874

Pitman Publishing Ltd
128 Long Acre
London
WC2E 9AN
01-379 7383

Plexus Computers Ltd
16 Cherry Orchard West
Kembrey Park
Swindon
Wiltshire
SN2 6UY
0793 614110/Turnkey/OA/ACC/APG/
COM/DAT/SD/WP/

Plusmark Business Systems
54 Moorbridge Road
Maidenhead
Berkshire SL7 8BN
0628 74661/Turnkey/FIN/ACC/

PMS Developments
Wetherwood Road
Rotherwas Industrial Estate
Hereford
HR2 6JU
0432 265768/Turnkey/PROD/MAN/

Policy Master Ltd
8 King Edwards Court
King Edwards Square
Sutton Coldfield
West Midlands
B72 1XS
021-355 3567

Positive Software
Almeley
Hereford
HR3 6RD
054 46 777

Powerscourt Ltd
Foundation House
Norreys Drive
Maidenhead
Berkshire
SL6 4BX
0628 771707/Turnkey/FIN/ACC

Praxis Systems plc
20 Manvers St
Bath
Avon
BA1 1PX
0225 335855

Precision Software
6 Park Terrace
Worcester Park
Surrey KT4 7JZ
01-330 7166

Primagraphics Ltd
Melbourn Science Park
Melbourn
Royston
Herts
SG8 6EJ
0763 62041

Prime Computer (UK) Ltd
Primos House
2-4 Lampton Road
Hounslow
Middlesex
TW3 1JW
01-572 7400/COM/DAT/GRA/OA/SD/SYS/

Printers Association Business Systems
4 Bishops Farm Close
Oakley Green
Windsor
Berkshire
07535 56691

Prior Knowledge Systems Ltd
1-5 The Horsefair
Romsey
Hants
SO51 8EZ
0794 515522

Program Products (Marketing)Ltd
Tileman House
131 Upper Richmond Road
London
SW15 2TP
01-785 3055/Turnkey/DTP/

Prologic
1 Shortlands
Hammersmith
London
W6 8DR
01-741 1988

Protek
10 Grosvenor Place
London
SW1X 7HH
01-245 6844

Protosoft Ltd
PO Box 582
London
W9 2QL
01-289 1101

QA Computer Systems
Matrix House
Goodman St
Leeds
West Yorkshire
LS10 1PA
0532 444722

QDQ Systems Ltd
127 Science Park
Milton Road
Cambridge CB4 4SD
0223 440044/Turnkey/FIN/INV/

Qontel Ltd
St Marys House
16-20 High St
Maidenhead
Berks
SL6 1QH
0628 785161/INS/

Quadraton UK Ltd
77a Walton Street
London
SW3 2HT
01-584 8733

Quaestor Systems Ltd
Eel Pie Marine Centre
Eel Pie Island
Twickenham
Middlesex
TW1 3DY
01-891 3849

Quartz Ltd
Studio 5
Intec Two
Wade Road
Basingstoke
Hampshire
RG24 0NL
0256 463535/APG/DAT/FSS/GRA/OA/
SYS/

Quotel Insurance Services
GSI House
Stanhope Road
Camberley
Surrey
GU15 3PS
0276 62155/Turnkey/FIN/

Radius plc
Wykeland House
47 Queen Street
Hull
Humberside
HU1 1UU
0482   227181/Turnkey/MAN/MED/PROD/
SD/ACC/COM/DAT/

Ram Computer Services
Synergy House
Eldon Place
Bradford
W Yorkshire
BD1 3AN
0274 736455/Turnkey/DTP/FIN/SD/ACC/

Rapid Winners Ltd
Rapid House
Denmark Street
High Wycombe
Bucks
HP11 2ER
0494 26271

Raven Computers
28-32 Cheapside
Bradford
West Yorkshire
BD1 4JA
0274 309386

Realtime Package Systems Ltd
Wyvern House
46-48 High Street
Bognor Regis
West Sussex
PO21 1SP
0243 822511/Turnkey/DIS/FIN/

Real Time Systems Ltd
Viking House
Nelson St
Douglas
Isle of Man
0642 26021

Reapmead Ltd
Computer House
1 Lakeside Place
London Colney
Herts
0727 25952

Recall Data Services Ltd
Stanley House
Stanley Avenue
Wembley
Middlesex
HA0 7JB
01-900 1555/Turnkey/REC/

Redwood International
Chaucer House
4-6 Upper Malborough Road
St Albans
Herts
AL1 3UR
0727 40601

Relational Technology Ltd
Anchor House
15-19 Britten St
London
SW3 3TY
01-351 7722/APG/DAT/

Retailer Computing Ltd
26 Burney Street
Greenwich
London
SE10
01-858 3446

RFA Ltd
The Chapel
5 Salisbury Street
Cranbourne
Dorset BH21 5PU
07254 566

ROCC Computers Ltd
Kelvin Way
Crawley
West Sussex
RH10 2LY
0293 31211

Roundhill Computer Systems
Axholme
London Road
Marlborough
Wiltshire
SN8 1LR
0672 54675

Rubicon Computer Systems
Rubicon House
Lamdin Road
Bury St Edmunds
Suffolk
IP32 6NU
0284 5671/Turnkey/MAN/ACC/

Runtime Systems Ltd
25a Rutland Square
Edinburgh
Scotland
EH1 2BW
031-228 3532

Ryan-McFarland Corporation
Crown House
Turners Hill
Cheshunt
Waltham Cross
Herts
EN8 8NN
0992 24981

Safe Computing
89-91 High Street
Leicester
LE1 4JB
0533 29321

Samna International
South Bank House
Black Prince Road
London
SE1 7SJ
01-587 1121/WP/

SAMS Ltd
Triangle House
198 Kettering Road
Northampton
NN1 4BL
0604 259131

Sanderson Computers Ltd
Parkway House
Parkway Avenue
Sheffield
S9 4WA
0742 434373

Santa Cruz Operation
Croxley Centre
Hatters Lane
Watford
WD1 8YN
0923 816344/COM/DAT/FSS/SYS/SP/

Savant
2 New Street
Carnforth
Lancashire
LA5 9BX
0524 734505

Scientific Software Ltd
Rose Industrial Estate
54 Marlow Bottom
Marlow
Buckinghamshire
SL7 3ND
0628 890011/GRA/OA/

Semads Ltd
3-4 Hardwick Street
London
EC1R 4RY
01-837 7765/Turnkey/FIN/PUB/

Service In Informatics & Analysis Ltd
Ebury Gate
23 Lower Belgrave Street
London
SW1W 0NW
01-730 4544/Turnkey/SD/CAD/DAT/

Sheffield Micro Ltd
Rutland House
Rutland Park
Sheffield
S Yorkshire
S10 2PB
0742 630154/Turnkey/ENG/FIN/MAN/
PROD/ACC/DAT/

Sherwood Computel Ltd
Renslade House
Whitefield
Gloucester GL1 1PG
0452 500477

Shortlands Computing
Clyde House
Reform Road
Maidenhead
Berkshire SL6 8BU
0628 75227/ACC/

Siemens Ltd
St Catherines House
2 Hanworth Road
Feltham, Middlesex
TW13 5BA
0932 785691/CAD/COM/DAT/GRA/OA/
SD/SYS/

Silicon Graphics Ltd
The Litten
Newtown Road
Newbury
Berks
RG14 7BB
0635 37425

Sintrom Electronics Ltd
14 Arkwright Road
Reading
Berks
RG2 0LS
0734 875464

Sirdar Data Systems Ltd
PO Box 31
Flanshaw Lane
Wakefield
West Yorkshire WF2 9ND
0924 375031

SK Computer Systems Ltd
St Michaels House
Norton Way South
Letchworth
Herts
SG6 1PB
0462 679331/Turnkey/OA/ACC

Skytronics Ltd
Chanpress House
59 Turney Street
Nottingham
Notts
NG2 2LG
0602 864350/ACC/COM/MAN/OA/TRN/

Slinn Computer Group Ltd
The Grange
Church St
Dronfield
Sheffield
South Yorkshire
S18 6QB
0246 412082/Turnkey/FIN/MAN/APG/

SMB Business Software Ltd
99 Staines Road West
Sunbury-on-Thames
Middlesex
TW16 7AH
0932 785566/ACC/MAN/

SM Computers Ltd
Newlands
Inglemire Lane
Hull
Humberside
0482 803591

Softech Professional Systems
9 Tonbridge Chambers
Pembury Road
Tonbridge
Kent
TN9 2HZ
0732 362688

Software Ireland
26 Linehall St
Belfast
N Ireland
BT2 8JP
0232 247433/SD/SYS/

Software Sciences Ltd
Meudon Avenue
Farnborough
Hampshire
GU14 7NB
0252 554321/Turnkey/PR//

Software Solutions
94A Norden Road
Maidenhead
Berkshire SL6 4BQ
0628 781135/DAT/

Sophos Ltd
20 Hawthorn Way
Kidlington
Oxfordshire
OX5 1EZ
0865 853668/SYS/

Sord Computer Corporation
12-14 Whitfield St
London W1
01-631 0787

Southdata
Voysey House
Barley Mow Passage
London W4 4PT
01-995 7587/Turnkey/DAT/

Special Software Ltd
Kipscombe
The Old Stables
Ingestre
Staffs
ST18 0RE
0889 271027

Sperry Ltd
Sperry Centre
Stonebridge Park
London
NW10 8LS
01-965 0511

Sphinx Ltd
43-53 Moorbridge Road
Maidenhead
Berkshire
SL6 8PL
0628 75343/COM/GRA/OA/SYS/

Spider Systems Ltd
65 Bonnington Road
Edinburgh
Lothian
EH6 5JQ
031-554 9197/COM/

SPSS UK Ltd
Mark House
Hersham Green
9-11 Queens Road
Walton-on-Thames
Surrey KT12 5LU
0932 232313/DAN/

SSI Ltd
Fordbrook Business Centre
Marlborough Road
Wiltshire
SN9 5NU
0672 63000

Star Computer Group
64 Great Eastern Street
London
EC2A 3QR
01-739 7633/Turnkey/FIN/OA/

Statistical Software Ltd
Cork Farm Centre
Dennehys Cross
Cork
County Cork
Republic of Ireland
0001 21 42722/DAN/

Status Software
373 Anlaby Road
Hull
North Humberside
HU3 6AB
0482 565306

STC Data Systems
Holbrook House
Cockfosters Road
Barnet
London
EN4 0DU
01-440 4141

Steam Radio Ltd
1 Perren Street
London
NW5 3ED
01-267 2561

Stella Computer Services
Pasture Lane
Ruddington
Nottingham
NG11 6AJ
0602 216949

Stewart Computer Systems
Systems House
2-6 Bridgford Road
West Bridgford
Nottingham
NG2 6AD
0602 815593/ACC/MAN/SYS/

Strategic Software
6/7 Benjamin Street
London
EC1M 5QL
01-608 0818

Stukeley Computer Services
Stukeley House
Barn Hill
Stamford
Lincs
PE9 2AE
0780 64947/Turnkey/LEG//

Style Systems Ltd
Style House
30 Adelaide Terrace
Blackburn, Lancashire
BB2 6ET
0254 51051

Subject Software Ltd
Crown House
Hartley Wintey
Basingstoke
Hampshire
RG27 8NW
0251 263706

Supported Systems Ltd
DP 74 Dean Clough Office Park
Dean Clough
Halifax
West Yorkshire
HX3 5AX
0442 48441/Turnkey/FIN/CON/ACC/DAT/
WP

Sydney Communications Ltd
Victoria House
Victoria Road
Aldershot
Hampshire
GU11 1EJ
0252 343100/COM/SYS/

Sydney Ltd
SPS House
40 Broadgate
Beeston
Nottingham NG9 2FW
0602 222227/COM/

Symicron Ltd
Charles House
35 Widmore Road
Bromley
Kent BR1 1RW

Symsys Ltd
50 Mill Lane
Lymm
Cheshire
WA13 9SQ
0925 756789/SD/

Synectic Computer Systems
10-12 High Street
Burnham
Buckinghamshire
SL1 7JH
06286 67070/DAT/

Synergy Logistics
Synergy House
Lisle Street
Loughborough
Leics
0509 232706

Sysmatic Ltd
Arkwright Road
Reading
Berks
RG2 0LS
0734 311011

Sysnet Ltd
50 Talbot Road
Talbot Green
Mid Glamorgan
CF7 8AF
0443 225247

Syspro (UK) Ltd
Dammas House
Dammas Lane
Swindon
Wiltshire
SN1 3EJ
0793 618130

Systemics Ltd
21-23 The Bridge
Middlesex
HA3 5AG
01-863 0079/ACC

Systems & Telecoms Ltd
Phoenix House
1 Station Hill
Reading
Berkshire
RG1 1NB
0734 500451/COM/

Systems Designers Ltd
Haw Bank House
High St
Cheadle
Stockport
Cheshire SK8 1AL
061-428 0811

System Simulation
Southbank House
Black Prince Road
London SE1 7SJ
01-582   3694/Turnkey/RET/SD/DAT/GRA/
SYS/

Systems Marketing Ltd
8-10 West Mills
Newbury
Berkshire
RG14 5HJ
0635 36111/SYS/

Systems Team Development Ltd
Merchants House
Merchants Landing
Bristol
BS1 4RW
0272 266281/ACC/

Systems Union Ltd
34 Delancey Street
Camden Town
London NW1 7NH
01-485 2594/ACC/OA/

Systime Computers Ltd
Leeds Business Park
Morley
Leeds
LS27 0NH
0532 529292/SYS/

Tab Shop
36 York Way
London
N1 9AB
01-278 9476

Tadpole Technology plc
Cambridge Science Park
Milton Road
Cambridge
Cambs CB4 4BH
0223 861112

Tagus Computer Systems Ltd
Southpoint
South Accommodation Road
Leeds LS10 1PP
0532 438210

Tangram CAD Ltd
Greyfriars Business Centre
2 Eaton Road
Coventry CV1 2SB
0203 520111

TCS Software
1 Nottingham Road
Melton Mowbray
Leics LE13 0NP
0664 500423

Team Computer Systems
Team House
High Street
Syston
Leicester LE7 8GP
0533 601874

Techmand Ltd
Slipway House
Eel Pie Island
Twickenham
Surrey
TW1 3DY
01-891 0086

Technology Concepts Ltd
Raglan House
Llantarnam Park
Cymbran
Gwent NP44 3AB
06333 72611/COM/

Tetra Business Systems
Foundation House
Norreys Drive
Maidenhead
Berks SL6
0628 770939/ACC/

Text Management Services Ltd
105 Fitzwilliam St
Huddersfield
HD1 5PS
0484 510178

Textronic UK Ltd
Fourth Avenue
Globe Park
Marlow
Buckinghamshire
SL7 1YD

The Accounting House Group
Yateley Lodge
Reading Road
Yateley
Camberley
Surrey
GU17 7AA
0252 877584/DAT/INV/

The Instruction Set Ltd
City House
190 City Road
London
EC1 2QH
01-251 2128

The Micro Solution Ltd
Park Farm House
Heythrop
Chipping Norton
Oxfordshire
OX7 5TW
0608 41197/MAN/

The Square Mile Co Ltd
Minerva House
26-27 Hatton Gardens
London EC1L 3BR
01-831 7090/Turnkey/FIN/

Thinking Software
Manchester Science Park
Lloyd St North
Manchester M15 4EN
061-226 0140

Thomson Computers Ltd
Marsters House
43 Blossom Street
York
YO2 2AQ
0904 611666/APG/SD/ACC/

Tibor Darvas Ltd
34 Pearce Road
Maidenhead
Berkshire
SL6 7LF
0628 25993/PCB/CAD/

Timberlake Clark Ltd
40b Royal Hill
Greenwich
London SE10 8RT
01-692 6636/7

TIS Group of Companies
St Marks House
1 Station Road
Bourne End
Buckinghamshire
SL8 5QF
06825 24999
Turnkey/TRA/CON/DTP/DIS/FIN/LEG/
MAN/MED/OA/PRT/PROD/PROP/REC/
RET/SM/SD/APG/DAT/GRA/TRN/WP/

TMB Computer Services
TMB House
Main Road
Nutbourne
W Sussex
PO18 8RL
0243 377421

TML Business Systems Ltd
3 High Street
Marlow, Bucks
SL7 1AU
06284 2165

Topas International
Lacemaker House
Chapel Street
Marlow
Buckinghamshire
SL7 3HQ
06284 75111/Turnkey/DIS/FIN/ACC/
MAN/

Tracline (UK) Ltd
Bennet House
1 High St
Edgware
Middlesex
HA8 7TH
01-952 7770

Transaction Point Ltd
Stuart House
43-47 Crown Street
Reading
Berks RG1 2SN
0734 866276

Triad Computing Systems Ltd
42 Kingsway
London
WC2B 6EX
01-831 7211/BES/Turnkey/SD/

Trio Computing
Harvest House
Paddock Road
Caversham
Reading
Berkshire RG4 6BY
0734 474766

Trisys Software Ltd
20 Poole Hill
Bournemouth
Dorset BH2 5PS
0202 291178/OA/

TSL Computer Group
Enterprise House
Manchester University Science Park
Lloyd Street North
Manchester
Greater Manchester
M15 4EN
061-226 0140/Turnkey/SM/APG/

Tudor Business Systems
Mill House
Mill Lane
Broom
Nr Bidford-on-Avon
Warwickshire
B50 4HS
0789 773737

Turnkey & Applied Systems
37-39 Bowling Green Lane
London
EC1R 0BJ
01-278 6426

UCC (Great Britain) Ltd
344-350 Euston Road
London
NW1 3BJ
01-387 9661

UCL Information Systems
3 Jefferson Way
Thame
Oxfordshire
OX9 3SU
084421 3151/OA/

UCSS Ltd
1 The Green
Marlborough
Wiltshire
SN8 1JA
0672 55315/ACC/FSS/MAN/OA/SYS/
FLT/WP

Unibit (Holdings) plc
20-26 Campus Road
Bradford
West Yorkshire
BD7 1HR
0274 736766/EXP/

Uniflex Software Ltd
Albany House
121 High Street
Crawley
Sussex
RH10 1DQ
0293 548369

Unify Corporation
Haleworth House
Tite Hill
Egham
Surrey
TW20 0LT
0784 71021/APG/

Unigram Products Ltd
4th Floor
12 Sutton Row
London
W1V 5FH
01-439 1632

Uniplex Ltd
Chaucer House
4-6 Upper Malborough Road
St Albans
Herts AL1 3UR
0727 40601/GRA/OA/

Unique Solutions Ltd
17-21 Castle Street
Cardiff
Wales
CF1 2BT
0222 390714

Unisoft Ltd
Saunderson House
Hayne St
London
EC1A 9HH
01-606 7799/ACC/DAT/MAN/OA/SD/WP/

Unisys
North Circular Road
Stonebridge Park
London
NW10 8LS
01-965 0511/APG/DAT/DTP/OA/SD/WP/

Unisystems Software Ltd
43 Upper Wickham Lane
Welling
Kent
DA16 3AJ
01-304 3902/COM/GRA/SD/SYS/FIN/

Unit-C Ltd
Dominion Way West
Broadwater
Worthing
Sussex
0903 205233

United Professional Systems
Bristol House
Victoria Street
Bristol
BS1 6BY
0272 276140/PAY/

UNIX Europe
27a Carlton Drive
London
SW15
01-785 6972

Unixsys (UK) Ltd
The Genesis Centre, Garrett Field
Science Park
South Birchwood
Warrington
Cheshire WA3 7BH
0925 828181/DTP/WP

Userlink Systems
9 Brabyns Brow
Marple
Stockport
Cheshire
SK6 7DA
061-427 7432

VT Computers Ltd
Unit 4
Airport Trading Estate
Biggin Hill
Westerham
Kent
TN16 3BW
0959 71933

Valid (UK) Ltd
Valid House
39 Windsor Road
Slough
Berks
SL1 2EE
0753 820101/CAD/

Vega Computers Ltd
6 Suffolk House
George Street
Croydon
Surrey
CR0 1PE
01-680 4484

Verwood Systems
Verwood House
High St
W Haddon
Northants
NN6 7AP
0788 87 629

VHA Computer Services
Coal Road
Leeds
West Yorks
LS14 2AL
0532 732442/Turnkey/PRT//

Vickers Communications
Graeme House
Wilbraham Road
Chorlton-cum-Hardy
Manchester
M21 1BU
061-861 9616

Vivaway Ltd
36-38 John Street
Luton
Beds
LU1 2JE
0582 423425

Vixon Computers
49 Grimsby Road
Cleethorpes
South Humberside
0472 58561

Wadale Associates Ltd
PO Box 33
Twickenham
Middlesex
TW1 4QG
01-686 5602

Walker Fisher PR Ltd
23 Rectory Grove
Croydon
Surrey
CR0 4JA
01-686 5602

Warren Point International
Babbage Road
Stevenage
Herts
SG1 2EQ
0438 316311

Warwick Computers Ltd
Warwick House
11 Newtown Road
Nuneaton
Warwickshire
CV11 4HR
0203 328967

Wayne Kerr Datum Ltd
Jenner Road
Crawley
West Sussex
RH10 2GA
0293 54911/Turnkey/TRN/CAD/

Weirlord Ltd
Unit 117
Somers Road North
Portsmouth
Hampshire
PO1 1PJ
0705 828035

Westborough Computer Services
Unit 3D
Newlands Centre
Inglemire Lane
Hull
Humberside
GU6 7TQ
0482 801559

Wharfedale Data Systems Ltd
Stanningley Industrial Centre
Varley Street
Pudsey
West Yorkshire
LS28 6AN
0532 557577/Turnkey/DIS/ACC/

William Lowe Associates
226 Cotterells
Hemel Hempstead
Hertfordshire
HP1 1JP
0442 47372/Turnkey/DIS//

Willow Ltd
Willow House
Gundrymoor Trading Estate
West Moors
Wimborne
Dorset
BH21 6QH
0202 861811/BAC/COM/GRA/OA/

Wootton Jeffreys Systems Ltd
72 Farnborough Road
Farnborough
Hampshire
GU14 6TH
0252 543098

XI Data Systems
Ladywise House
Parkfield Street
Leeds
West Yorkshire
LS11 5PH
0532 452788

Xi Software Ltd
47 Cedarwood Drive
St Albans
Herts
AL4 0DN
0727 57267/DAT/SYS/

Xitan Systems
Xitan House
27 Salisbury Road
Totton
Southampton
Hampshire
SO4 3HX
0703 871211

X-ON Software
65 Victoria Road
London
N22 4XA
01-881 3659

Xoren Computing Ltd
28 Maddox Street
London
W1R 9PF
01-629 5932

Xylogics International Ltd
2a Cofferidge Close
Stony Stratford
Milton Keynes
Buckinghamshire
MK11 1BY
0908 569444

Zircon Ltd
PO Box 85
Crawley
West Sussex
RH10 2YL
0293 23631